Gwathmey Siegel & Associates Architects

Selected and Current Works

Gwathmey Siegel & Associates Architects

Selected and Current Works

First published in Australia in 1998 by
The Images Publishing Group Pty Ltd
ACN 059 734 431
6 Bastow Place, Mulgrave, Victoria, 3170
Telephone (61 3) 9561 5544 Facsimile (61 3) 9561 4860

National Library of Australia Cataloguing-in-Publication Data

Gwathmey Siegel & Associates Architects
Gwathmey Siegel & Associates Architects: selected and current works.

Bibliography.
Includes index.
ISBN 1 875498 74 5.

1. Gwathmey Siegel & Associates Architects. 2. Architecture, American.
3. Architecture, Modern—20th century—United States.
I. Title. (Series: Master architect series 3).

720.973

Edited by Stephen Dobney
Designed by The Graphic Image Studio Pty Ltd,
Mulgrave, Australia
Film by Scanagraphix Australia Pty Ltd
Printed in Hong Kong

Contents

INTRODUCTION

Introduction

By Charles Gwathmey

"Vision is the art of seeing things invisible."
Jonathan Swift

In America, modern architects are still confronting a time in history when art and culture are at a crossroads. There are two competing possibilities: the first is an enriched extension of our Modernist culture; the second is the entrenchment of the populist Post-Modernist culture. The former is intellectually and morally acceptable; the latter, I believe, is not.

Modernism, as we know it, has served as the aesthetic, spiritual, and moral conscience of our time. It has also been the preeminent representative, intellectually, of our democratic society. The Modernist ideal has been predicated on the invention of a personal style, as an aesthetic, linked to the conception of a unique self, generating a unique vision of the world. It fosters a dynamic intellectual climate, based upon the obligation to interrogate, to analyze, to criticize in the exhaustive process of "finding truth," not for pleasure, convenience, or expedient confirmation, but as a life exercise. The demands are relentless; the search is painstaking; the results, more often than not, are transitional. The alternative, however, is intellectual apathy and creative atrophy.

Imagine the void without Picasso or Giocometti, Proust or T.S. Eliot, Le Corbusier, Mies van der Rohe or Frank Lloyd Wright, or, in our time, Kahn, Stirling, Foster, Rogers, Ando, Gehry, Meier, Hejduk, and Eisenman.

The idea of "Modernism" is not new. However, it has been severely assaulted—by artists and critics, theorists and philosophers, journalists and political activists—to the degree that what is both essential and vital to the cultural life of our democratic society is being threatened.

It is interesting to note that present day Modernism established itself as part of mainstream culture during the 1960s, in the Kennedy era, and was initially assaulted after his assassination, reaching its point of crisis during the 1980s, coinciding with the re-election of President Reagan. What we are now witnessing, with exceptions of course, is the historic breakdown in the divisions which once separated radicals from conservatives and the avant-garde from the Philistines. It is still, unfortunately, a time of self-satisfaction, preservation, habit, and an unwillingness to endorse exploration, which requires both risk and the willingness to "fail." Only in that climate can we discover, and thus enrich, the art and the culture.

A most poignant observation, and one that summarizes this state, was expressed by Mario Vargas Llosa: "in order to live harmoniously in society, man has had to mutilate himself, to repress his most formidable, but asocial desires and extravagant fantasies. The state is the political expression of the repression and, as such, is a necessary evil: it protects us from ourselves. Literature provides a compensation for these repressed feelings. It is an arena where man's fantasies can safely unfold themselves, uncensored by the demands of social life. In this sense, literature can be said to have a subversive function by articulating desires that are at odds with the prevailing social order. It challenges the dominance of that order. But in many societies, especially in democratic ones, this subversive function seems to have lost its edge. Increasingly, literature has become little more than a form of entertainment."

I submit that this also aptly applies to Post-Modern art and architecture. A "post-Modern" culture, based upon historicism, revisionism, traditionalism, preservationism, and conservatism, engenders a climate of intellectual stagnation, false security, and perceptual passivity, while simultaneously fertilizing, behind the facade or the academic gown, corruption, deceit, arrogance, and decadence—all seeds of destruction.

The Israeli writer Amos Oz observed, "Whoever ignores the existence of varying degrees of evil is bound to become a servant of evil."

The preferred rationale of "representationalism," the byword of Post-Modernism (as opposed to abstraction), is that it is pleasurable, comprehensible, picturesque, and thus universally accessible. However, it denies the inherent obligations of art: to seek an essence of meaning; to embody ideas; to reduce preconceptions; and to probe, speculate, and ultimately, provoke new perceptions, as well as new awareness.

In that regard, I refer to our addition to the Guggenheim Museum, by Frank Lloyd Wright, which was systematically attacked by preservationists and historians alike. It did not seem to be a rational reaction, but one based upon protectivism and misguided sentimentality. When Wright unveiled his design in 1952, he was castigated, ostracized, belittled, and labeled an iconoclast; today he is revered, respected, protected, and sacrosanct. The opportunity to design the addition was compelling and challenging. To have turned it down would have been a contradiction. More importantly, it would also have denied precedent. The history of architecture has always supported intervention, dialogue, counterpoint, and theory. Architecture is not static; nor is perception. I believe in the idea of the addition, as much as in the integrity of our design. In the end, and consistent with my passions, I could not accept the heresy of an architectural or intellectual status quo.

Research for information to provoke redefinition, reinterpretation, or rejection is positive. Research to justify the known and maintain the status quo is negative. Architects create art not by re-establishing the established or representing the presented, but by creating new meanings of form and space through investigation and experimentation.

Picasso and Braque relentlessly pursued an investigation of perceptual alternatives that forever changed our way of seeing: Cubism.

Our work demonstrates a research and discovery process based upon formal structures and reductive editing that, in the more inventive realizations, represents a sense of essence and density that we hope endures.

SELECTED AND CURRENT WORKS

Solomon R. Guggenheim Museum Addition, Renovation, and Restoration

Design/Completion 1982/1992
New York, New York
The Solomon R. Guggenheim Foundation
30,000 square feet (addition); 120,000 square feet (renovation)
Prefabricated limestone panels on steel trusses, painted aluminum, glass, glass block, stainless steel, bronze, glass fiber, reinforced concrete columns
Painted gypsum; painted plaster; sand bed, precast, and epoxy terrazzo; opaque glass; metal panels; stainless steel and bronze doors and railings

The program included the renovation and restoration of the Frank Lloyd Wright museum and a 30,000-square-foot addition to the original building.

The parti for the addition was determined by its two critical intersections with the original building: with the rotunda at the existing circulation core, and with the monitor building along its east wall. At the triangular stair, the addition provides balcony views and access to the rotunda from three new two-story galleries and one single-story gallery. The hinge/knuckle stair is experienced from the new galleries as both a space and an object. The transparent glass wall between the monitor building and the addition reveals the original facades from the outside in and the inside out. The rotunda becomes a "courtyard/cloister" space for both the addition and the monitor building.

The second floor of the monitor building was renovated as a gallery in 1954, establishing a precedent for the spatial interconnection between the monitor building and the large rotunda. This precedent was extended by converting each floor of the monitor building into exhibition space and by integrating the pavilions, functionally and spatially, with the large rotunda as well as with the new addition. The interconnected pavilions offer views to Central Park and to the skylit

Continued

1 View from Fifth Avenue

1

small rotunda, a counterpoint to the large rotunda. Outside, the new fifth-floor roof sculpture terrace, the large rotunda roof terrace, and the renovated public ramp from the street to the auditorium reveal the original building in a new, extended, and comprehensive perspective.

In the rotunda, numerous technical refinements have corrected omissions in the original construction and brought the building up to current museum standards. The reglazing of the central lantern, the re-opening of the clerestories that run between the turns of the spiral wall, and the restoration of the scalloped flat clerestory at the perimeter of the ground floor exhibition space have restored the quality of light that was evident in the original design. The high gallery set the original precedent for leaving and re-entering the ramp/rotunda. Each ramp cycle now affords the option of entry or views to new galleries. Most significantly, the extension of the uppermost ramp of the rotunda, which had been closed to the public since it was built, creates alternative circulation back to the ground floor and provides a culmination to this major public space for the first time.

2

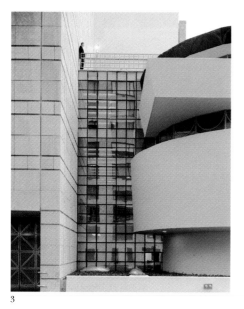

3

4

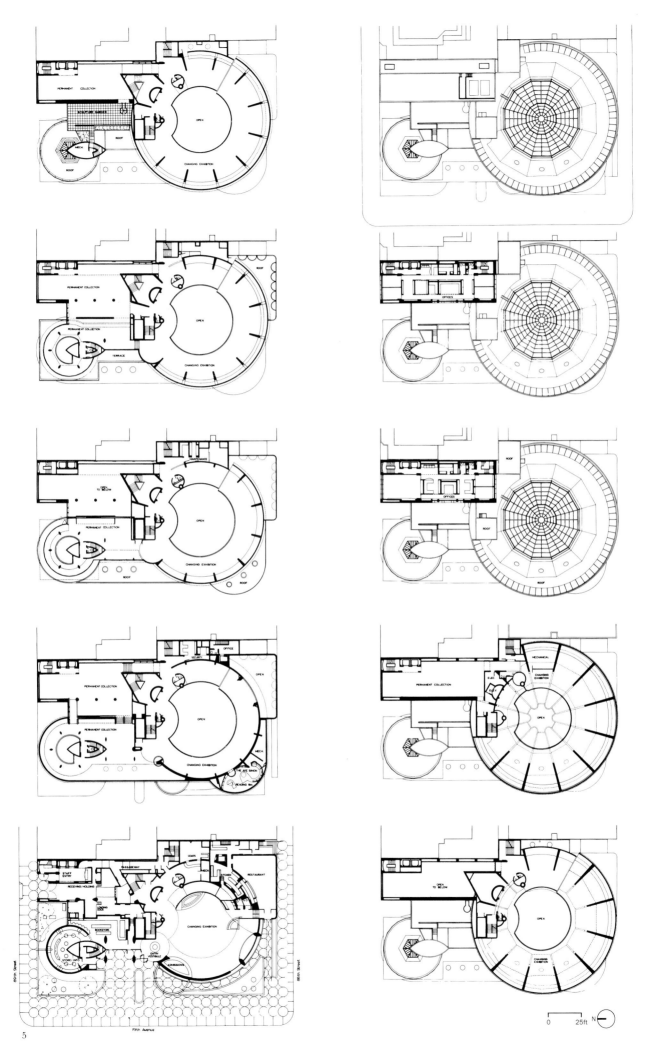

5

Solomon R. Guggenheim Museum Addition, Renovation, and Restoration   19

6 New fifth and sixth level gallery with access to roof terrace
7 New second and third level gallery with Thannhauser gallery beyond
8 Fourth level gallery in monitor building with reconstructed cornice
9 Renovated seventh level ramp in large rotunda

6

7

8

9

American Museum of the Moving Image

Design/Completion 1983/1988
Astoria, New York
American Museum of the Moving Image
55,000 square feet
Painted concrete, aluminum, single-ply ballasted roofing

This specialized museum is housed in a three-story 1920s concrete loft building, adjacent to the Astoria Moving Picture Studio Complex. The existing window openings were reglazed and the stucco exterior masonry repaired, as required by the National Registration of Historic Buildings.

Located on the ground floor are the flexible exhibition gallery, a state-of-the-art 200-seat movie theater, a bookstore/museum shop, and the lobby and cafe area. On the second floor are administrative offices, a multi-use exhibition loft, and the Movie Palace. The third floor and roof pavilion provide exhibition and entertainment space.

The new stair and elevator tower, located in the courtyard beyond the original facade and on axis with the main entrance, reads as a counterpointal object to the original frame. Landings provide visitors with a heightened visual experience before re-entering the exhibition spaces in the original building.

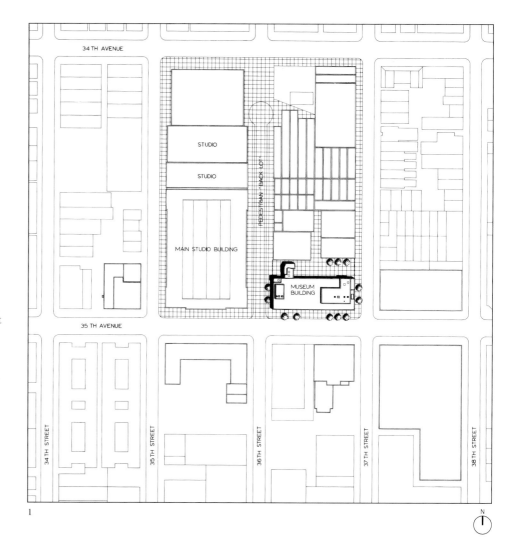

1

1   Site plan
2   Landmarked facade of renovated building
3   View of new stair tower from courtyard

2

4

5

4   View of new stair tower from courtyard
5   View of new stair tower at dusk
6   Stair tower detail

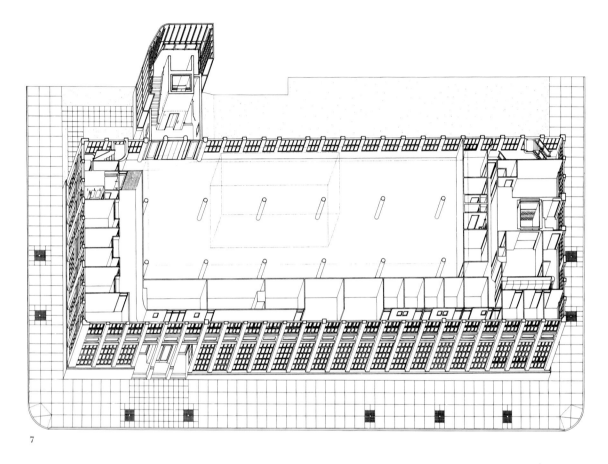

7

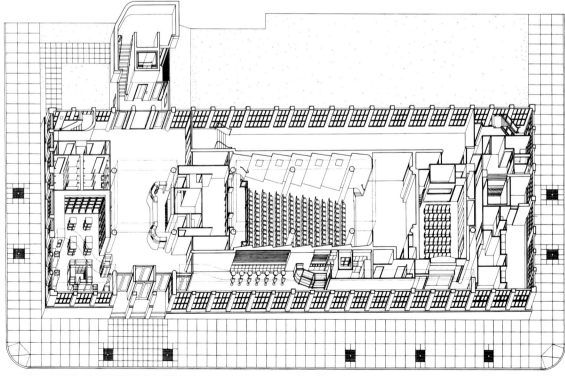

8

9

11

12

10

John W. Berry Sports Center, Dartmouth College

Design/Completion 1984/1988
Hanover, New Hampshire
Dartmouth College
118,000 square feet
Groundface concrete block, brick, stone, painted wood

This building addition is an expansion of the athletics facilities of the original Alumni Gymnasium. It is located within a traditional brick and stone Ivy League campus, and adjacent to athletics fields, tennis courts, and residential streets.

The ground floor houses a 2,200-seat intercollegiate basketball arena which reconfigures into a three-court gymnasium; a physical fitness center and classroom; varsity locker rooms; athletics ticket offices; and a concession area.

The second floor, reached by two stairs and a bridge from the renovated Alumni Gymnasium, houses seven competition squash courts, six racquetball courts, a dance studio, and spectator bleacher balconies. The facilities are accessed from a barrel-vaulted, skylit gallery, terminated by a bay window overlooking the entry.

Horizontal and vertical circulation elements wrap the three sides of the basketball arena, allowing natural light into the fitness center and dance studio. Exterior materials address contextual constraints and articulate the internal volumes as well as the layered organization of the plan.

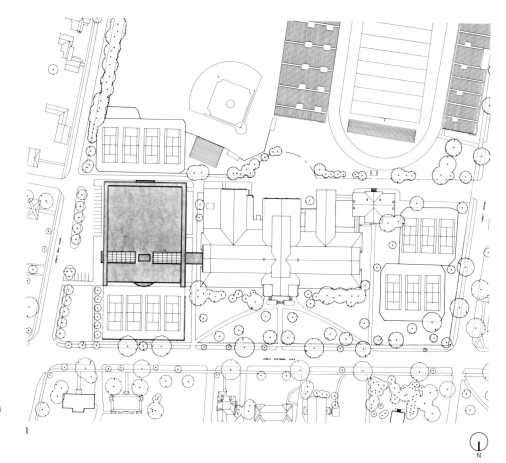

1

N

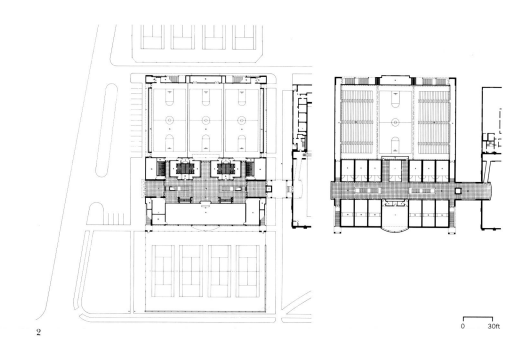

1   Site plan
2   Ground level plan
3   Upper level plan
4   View of public entry facade with gallery bay window above
5   View showing connection bridge from existing building
6   Rear elevation
7   Night view of north facade from tennis courts
8   Northwest corner of building from lawn

2

0   30ft

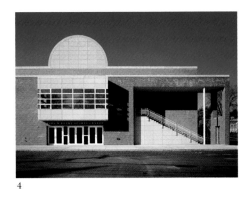

4

5

6

7

8

9   Three-glass-wall exhibition squash court
10&11 Basketball arena
12   Dance studio
13   North elevation
14   Spectator gallery for squash courts, showing stairs
       from lobby and bay window at end of gallery

9

10

11

12

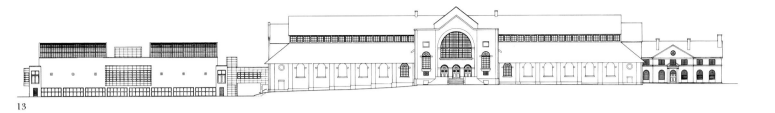

13

14

Cornell University Buildings

All three of these campus buildings—the Basketball Arena and Fieldhouse, the College of Agriculture, and the Computer Science Theory Center at the College of Engineering—share common elements. They are larger than adjacent buildings, they address the issue of edge and define major outdoor spaces, and they establish precedents for a master plan that supports the urban constraints of each site. Constructive interaction with the user groups, the facilities planners, and the administration was essential to the realization of these projects.

The College of Agriculture building closes the quadrangle at the end of its west axis. It forms a gateway from the south campus to Bailey Plaza, which has been redefined as an outdoor pedestrian court that anchors the main campus auditorium and adjacent structures. The Basketball Arena and Fieldhouse is an addition to the hockey rink that redefines the edge of the practice fields at the center of the north campus. The Computer Science Theory Center is contextually more complex than the other two buildings, as it borders a gorge that posed significant ecological constraints. It is located on the curve of Campus Road, facing the baseball field, and is diagonally opposite the football stadium and the existing fieldhouse, the two largest structures on campus.

With the completion of the three buildings, a precedent for Cornell University architecture was realized: buildings which are site-responsive, programmatically flexible, materially dense, and scale-sensitive. In their formal articulation, contextual interaction, and use of collage, these new structures are intended to be read simultaneously as extensions and transformations.

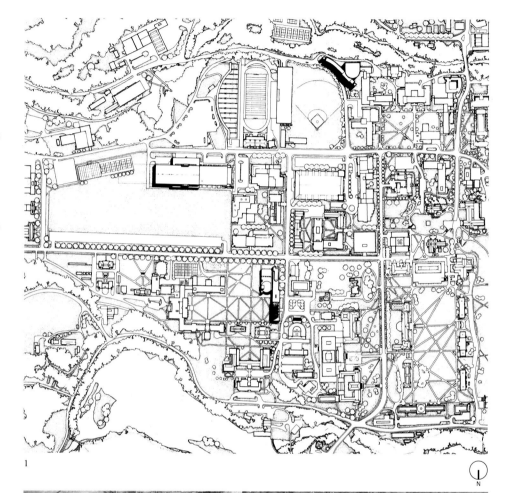

1

2

1 Site plan
2 Aerial view

Basketball Arena and Fieldhouse, Cornell University

Design/Completion 1985/1989
Ithaca, New York
Cornell University
180,000 square feet
Precast concrete, groundface concrete block, porcelain panels

This building forms the southern edge of Cornell's varsity practice fields. It consists of two major volumes: the basketball arena, with three regulation NCAA courts and roll-out seating for 5,000 spectators, and the fieldhouse cage.

When the two-tiered bleachers are extended, the three basketball courts merge to form a single exhibition court. A continuous balcony surrounds the space at the upper bleacher level. The court is overlooked by coaches' offices at one end and the bay window of the alumni lounge at the other. The cage is a large, naturally lit multipurpose practice space that includes a climbing wall for teaching and training.

The lobby is the organizational fulcrum of the building, linking the office service areas with the main athletics spaces and providing an interconnecting public entrance to the existing hockey rink.

Unlike the traditional campus model, the design clearly articulates the interior volumes that define the spatial, circulation, and organizational hierarchy of the building. At the same time it establishes an architectural presence from both the street and the practice fields.

1

2

3

1 North facade
2&3 Southwest facade

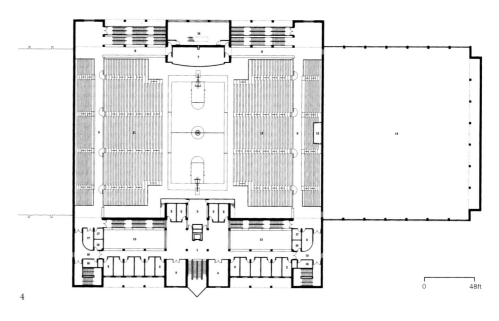

4

5

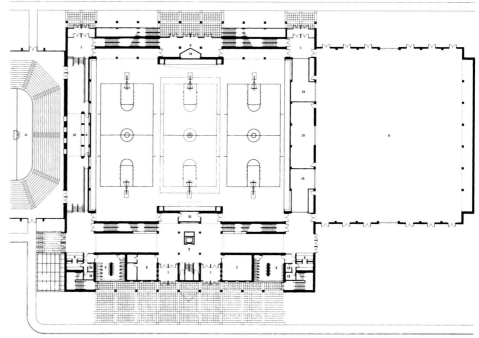

6

7

8

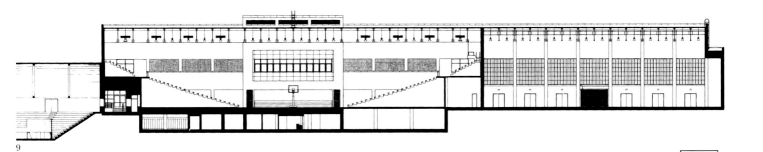

9

0   24ft

10

11

4   Second floor plan

5   Lobby and public stair

6   Entry floor plan

7   Entry arcade

8   Main stair

9   Longitudinal section

10   Basketball arena with expanding seats

11   Multipurpose fieldhouse cage with climbing wall

College of Agriculture and Life Sciences, Cornell University

Design/Completion 1984/1989
Ithaca, New York
Cornell University
140,000 square feet
Steel and concrete deck, brick, cast stone, teak wood windows and doors, curtain wall
Mahogany, terrazzo, plaster

The Agriculture Quadrangle was defined by five-story masonry buildings on three sides with an open, undefined end on Bailey Plaza. The new administrative building, fronting both Bailey Plaza and the Agriculture Quad, redefines Bailey Plaza as an urban space and the quadrangle as an enclosed outdoor room.

The building accommodates administrative offices on the first three floors and the Landscape Architecture School on the fourth floor. Crowning the building is a barrel-vaulted studio space with double-height windows facing the quadrangle, and a framed roof terrace facing Bailey Plaza. A connecting bridge provides access to the Landscape Department from the academic building and frames a three-story gate to the quadrangle that recalls similar college gates on the campus.

A primary pedestrian pathway from the quadrangle to the campus gate forms one of the main entrances to the academic building; the other is at the corner of Tower Road and Garden Avenue. A two-story gallery with balcony mezzanine is the primary interior circulation spine, connecting the two entrances and providing access to classrooms, a 600-seat lecture auditorium, and a 400-seat dining facility. The third and fourth floors of the building house faculty offices and teaching support space.

1

1 Entry gate from Bailey Plaza
2 Entry gate facade
3 East facade from quadrangle
4 Detail of entry gate
5 Entry to academic building from Tower Road

2

3

4

5

6

7

8

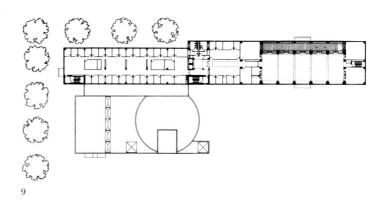

9

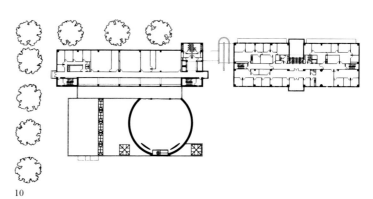

10

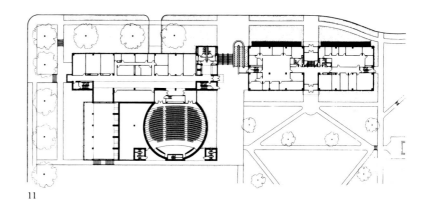

11

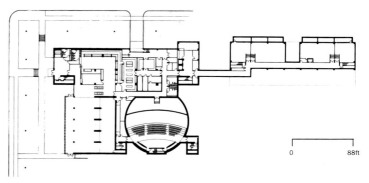

12

6 Detail
7 Dean's office overlooking quadrangle
8 Circulation gallery in academic building
9 Fourth level plan
10 Second level plan
11 Ground level plan
12 Basement level plan
13 Architecture studio
14 600-seat auditorium
15 Dining hall

0   88ft

13

14

15

Computer Science Theory Center, Cornell University

Design/Completion 1987/1990
Ithaca, New York
Cornell University
211,000 square feet
Steel and concrete deck, brick, cast stone, aluminum panels, curtain wall
Sheltrock, raised floor, painted block

This seven-story building is organized into two elements: a 300-foot-long serpentine office building and a larger cubical mass that houses high-tech computer rooms and column-free laboratories. The intersection of the office slabs at the lab block forms the entrance and service core, which includes meeting rooms, a fifth-level sky-lobby, and a reception area for the supercomputing group.

The building is the largest structure on the Engineering campus and is connected to two existing buildings on the quad by an elevated pedestrian walkway and an underground tunnel. The generic offices on the lower floors provide flexible space for future reconfigurations to accommodate changes in electronic and computer technology.

The design responds to severe site constraints by presenting a new gateway to the campus as well as establishing a new architectural reference for the north campus.

1

2

3

40

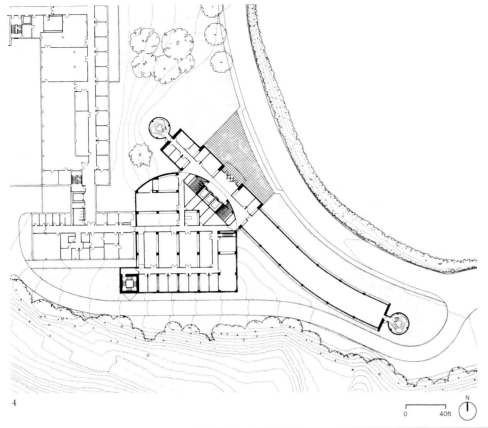

4

1   View from Barton Hall
2   Aerial view from Barton Hall
3   Laboratory building from gorge
4   Site plan
5   View of building from Campus Road

0   40ft   N

5

6 Computer classroom
7 Link from the new Engineering Building to the new Theory Center
8 Interior of stair tower
9 Corner detail, showing stair tower, office building, and laboratory building

6

7

8

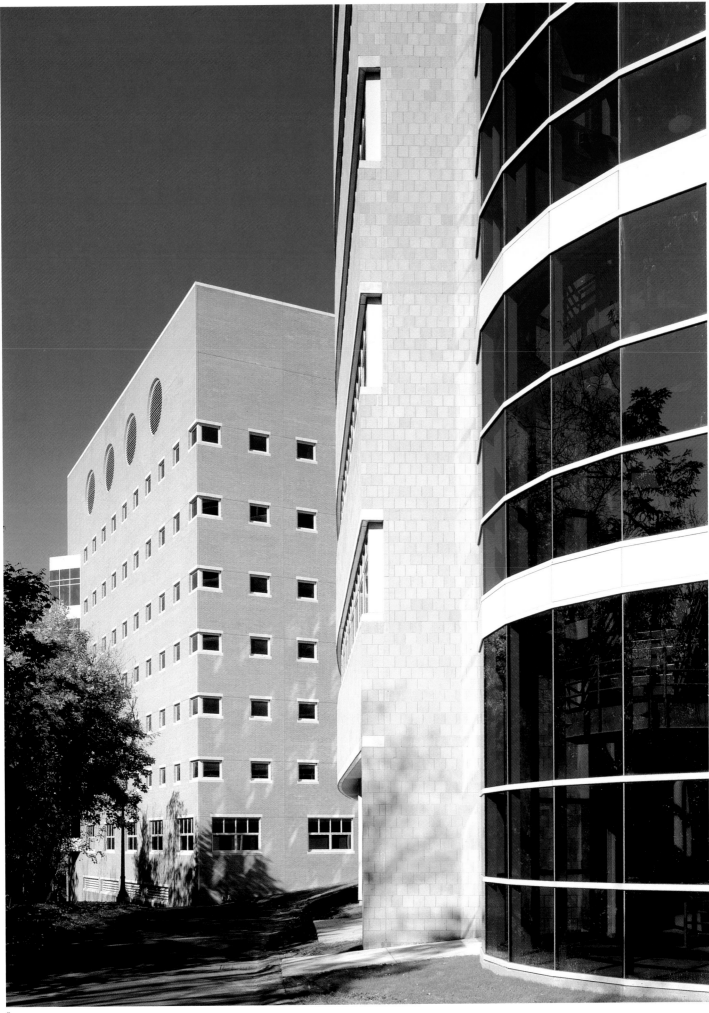

9

Knoll International Showroom

Design/Completion 1983/1986
Chicago, Illinois
Knoll International
18,000 square feet
Granite, stucco, structural glass panels, painted wood, spot fixtures

This design creates a permanent yet flexible environment for ever-changing displays of furniture, objects, and fabric. The showroom's uncompromising yet restrained design retains a timeless sense of presence while focusing attention on the quality of the exhibits.

The grid derives from the dimensional module of an existing central lightwell and two rows of columns. The lightwell was transformed from a transparent void into a solid volume of white glass, creating a fixed object against which continually changing products are displayed. Defined spaces line the perimeter, leaving an open plan between the gridded glass wall and the central white glass object. A suspended ceiling grid of painted wood accommodates multiple lighting sources and hangings, and maintains a unified but flexible visual plane over the entire space.

In addition to display space, the showroom accommodates staff offices, a kitchen, and storage, as well as a multi-use video presentation space.

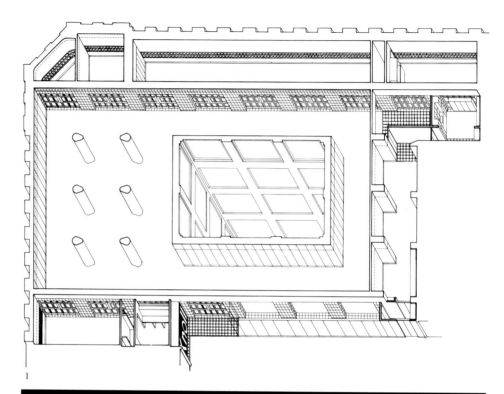

1

2

1   Axonometric
2   Entry from public gallery
Opposite:
    Showroom from entry

44

4

5

6

7

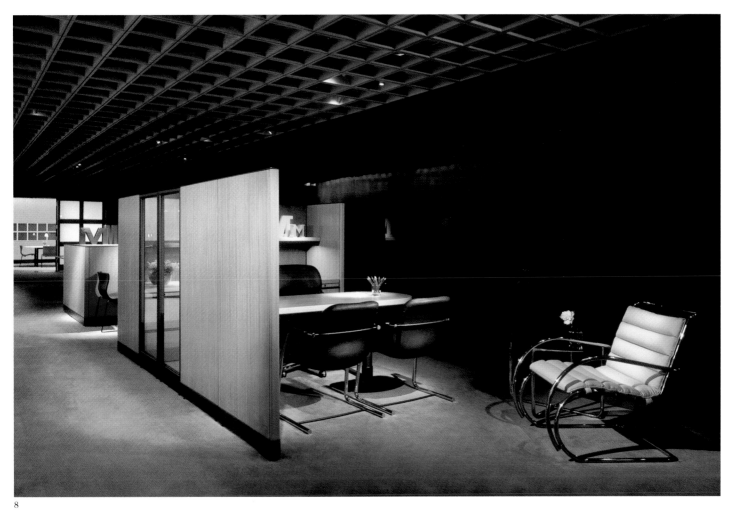

8

9

4   Showroom
5&6   Views of showrooms
7   Office interior showing panel wall
8   Typical office space
9   Conference room

IBM Corporation Office Building and Distribution Center

Design/Completion 1985/1987
Greensboro, North Carolina
IBM Corporation
150,000 square feet
Concrete, clear spandrel and frosted glass, glass block, ceramic tiles, porcelain panels

Located adjacent to a main highway, the building is organized to accommodate five floors of flexible office space. Expansion of the original structure is provided in two phases to the east and west.

The glass on the southern side is recessed behind the exposed concrete structure, creating an integrated sunscreen which redefines the sculptured facade. The entrance to the building is through the tower element, which contains a five-story atrium and the elevator system. Access to each floor is from a balcony overlooking the atrium with views to downtown Greensboro.

On the north, the glass is flush with the floor edge to create an opposite facade reading. Three types of glass—clear, spandrel, and frosted—are used to articulate floor, sill, and suspended ceiling data.

In contrast to the exposed concrete frame, the entrance tower is clad in white tiles, glass blocks, and white porcelain panels. The tower element is in counterpoint to the object/frame reading of the main structure, and also redefines the entry plaza and the landscape between building and parking area.

Using basic construction technology, this generic building type is transformed by innovative planning, structural clarity, and the use of integrated sunscreens that provide both environmental control and facade articulation.

1

1   Detail of metal grating between brise-soleil and glass window wall
2   Site plan
3   View of building from southwest
4   Night view of entry plaza lobby
5   Entry plaza to lobby

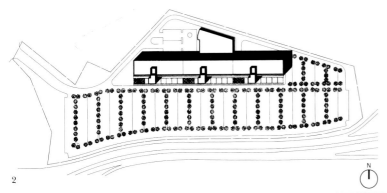

2

3

4

5

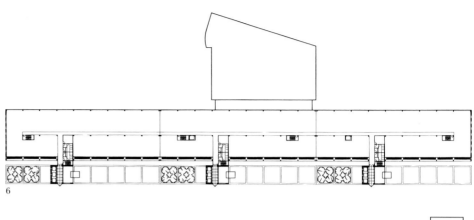

6

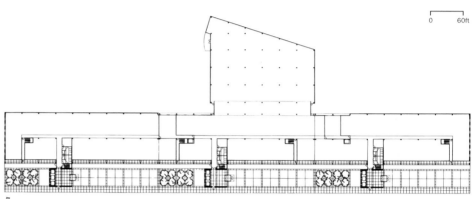

0   60ft

7

6   Typical floor plan
7   Ground floor plan
8   Porthole view from elevator stops
9   Lobby detail
10   View of typical elevator bridge
11   View from typical elevator bridge through lobby

8

9

10

11

East Academic Complex, Eugenio Maria de Hostos Community College

Design/Completion 1985/1994
Bronx, New York
City University of New York
240,000 square feet
Banded brick, white porcelain panels, glass, glass block, Kalwall, painted plaster, ceramic tiles, terrazzo

This multipurpose building for a community college in a Spanish-speaking area of the Bronx represents a composite program located in a dense urban context. The building program provides for classrooms, faculty and student offices, a swimming pool, a gymnasium and ancillary athletics spaces, a 1,200-seat proscenium theater, a 350-seat repertory theater, faculty and student dining facilities, a campus store, an art gallery and studios, and a pedestrian bridge linking existing campus buildings to the new structure.

The Grand Concourse facade reinforces the built edge, establishes a gateway to the college, and, together with the original campus structure, defines an outdoor courtyard. The new tower and bridge serve as visual icons, establishing a sense of place and a new image for the campus and the community

The building contains many departments with diverse and varied functions. As a unifying design strategy, it is organized around a five-story skylit atrium. Articulated horizontally with balconies and vertically with stairs, the atrium is the major public space on the campus. It is the primary internal circulation volume of the new building as well as providing lobby space for the repertory and proscenium theaters and access to the bridge.

1

1   View across Grand Concourse to the East Academic Complex
2   East Academic Complex and pedestrian bridge
3   Tower viewed from pedestrian bridge
4   Entry level plan
5   View of atrium from walkways
6   Atrium walkways
7   Main atrium

2

3

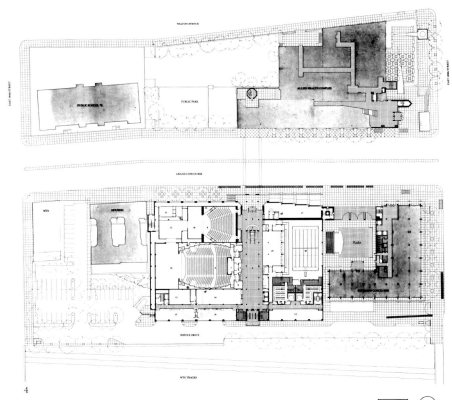

4

0   50ft   N

5

6

7

8

9

10

11

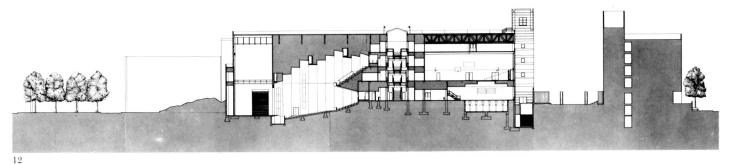

12

13

14

15

Morgan Stanley & Co. Inc., World Headquarters

Design/Completion 1985/1990
New York, New York
Morgan Stanley & Co. Inc.
1,300,000 square feet
Blue-green, white-patterned, and mirrored glass; silver-gray metallic
painted aluminum panels; polished stainless steel; green marble;
black and white granite; anagre wood panels and coffered ceilings

This tower is located in the Times Square area of midtown Manhattan. The diagonal, stepped base responds to the pedestrian scale of the street in the theater district. The segmented curve of the double-height mechanical floor signals the transition from the diagonal base to the orthogonal tower, which refers to the city grid. The building's articulated top creates a strong silhouette on the Manhattan skyline.

The curtain wall facade is composed of layers of glass and metal panels which give multiple readings of opacity and reflectivity with changes in the natural light.

Three levels of building signage respond to the zoning requirements of Times Square: at pedestrian level there are individual retail signs for each storefront; above these are 10 vertical, cantilevered fins in black glass which collectively spell "1585 B'way;" finally, above the first building setback, three horizontally scrolling electronic message boards carry stock market quotations and financial news. Large video panels, situated at each side street, display images and text towards upper Broadway and lower Times Square.

In 1995 the entry lobby was redesigned to provide for a new cafeteria below grade. The original floor plate was adapted to accommodate two sets of escalators, accessed from either side by a connecting bridge. The bridge offers views across the lobby through a curved glass wall, and below to the cafeteria area.

The 40th and 41st executive floors were also designed in 1995. They are connected by a double-height entry space which affords panoramic views over Manhattan and reads as a referential volume for the two floors.

1

1   View from New Jersey looking east across the
    Hudson River
2   Detail of building signage from Times Square
3   Pedestrian passage and auto drop-off
4   Main lobby

2

3

4

Morgan Stanley & Co. Inc., World Headquarters 57

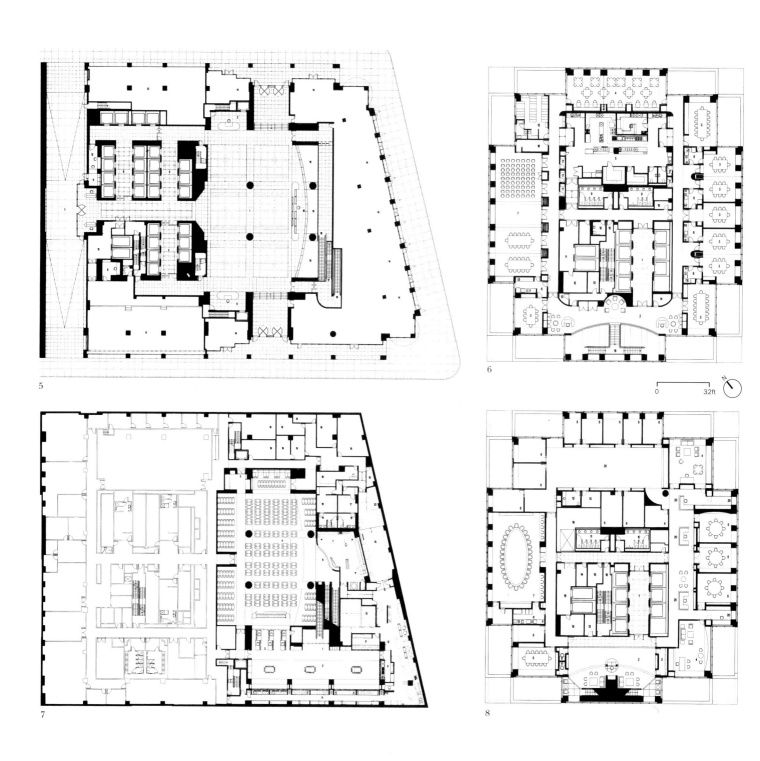

5

6

0   32ft   N

7

8

9

10

11

5 Lobby level floor plan
6 41st level floor plan
7 Lower level/cafeteria floor plan
8 40th level floor plan
9 Skylit arcade between main lobby and auto drop-off
10 Main lobby and cafeteria
11 Main cafeteria at basement level
12 Exit from cafeteria

12

Center for the Arts, State University of New York at Buffalo

Design/Completion 1985/1992
Amherst, New York
State University Construction Fund
264,000 square feet
Three colors of brick, painted white panels,
white painted aluminum doors and windows, Kalwall
Terrazzo floors and stairs at public areas, drywall,
acoustic tiles, painted metal doors and frames

The Center for the Arts is situated on the last open site at the State University of New York at Buffalo. Located at the end of the primary cross-axis of the campus, overlooking Lake LaSalle, the building redefines Coventry Circle as a major entry plaza for both athletics and performing arts events.

The building is asymmetrically bisected by a two-story skylit gallery that defines the north–south axis and connects the Fine Arts and Theater Arts departments. The Fine Arts Department consists of a student/faculty art gallery; sculpture, photography, drawing, and painting studios; and administrative and faculty offices.

The Theater Arts Department is larger, with an 1,800-seat full proscenium concert/opera theater, a 400-seat repertory theater, two rehearsal theaters, a screening room, a media department and studio, two dance studios, a full-service backstage area, and miscellaneous support spaces.

The art studios and performance spaces were designed to provide maximum flexibility for students and faculty. The combination of the two disciplines into a single building adds a programmatic and cultural dynamic to the center of the campus, increasing student and public access to the university's multidisciplinary activities.

To break down the scale, articulate the massing, and integrate the building into the existing context, horizontally banded brick of three colors and sizes is used as the primary exterior material, creating a counterpoint to the white painted aluminum panels that define the public volumes, circulation spaces, and stage houses.

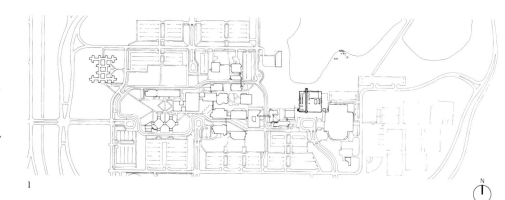

1

N

1 Site plan
2 View of public entrance and south facade from Coventry Circle
3 View of north facade overlooking Lake LaSalle
4 Detail of south facade
5 University art gallery seen from Coventry Circle

2

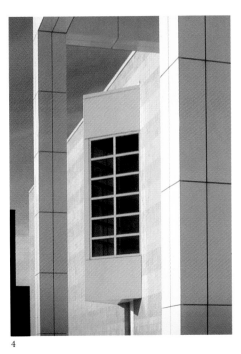

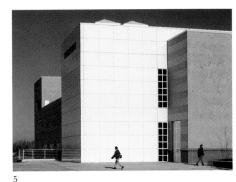

3

4

5

9

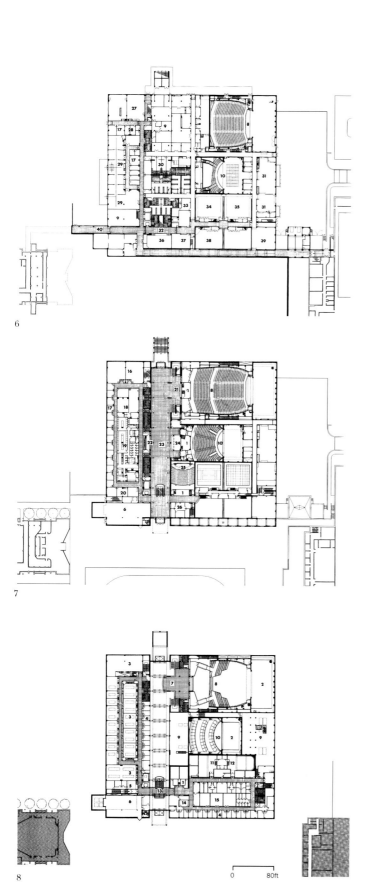

6

7

10

11

12

8

0   80ft

13

6   Lower floor plan
7   Entry floor plan
8   Upper floor plan
9   Orchestra and balcony lobbies by day
10 Atrium by night
11 Atrium by day
12 Atrium from balcony lobby
13 Dance studio with control room and balcony
    overlooking dance floor
14 400-seat drama theater
15 View from the stage of the main theater

14

15

Thomas I. Storrs Architecture Building, University of North Carolina at Charlotte

Design/Completion 1986/1989
Charlotte, North Carolina
University of North Carolina
83,000 square feet
Steel frame structure with masonry walls, groundfaced concrete block, brick, glazed tiles, Kalwall, aluminum windows and doors

The College of Architecture is the first building to be constructed on the perimeter of the campus, originally designed in the 1960s.

Sited on a former parking lot, the development set a precedent for the design of outdoor spaces between campus buildings and resolved the previously undefined campus circulation system by introducing a parking strategy that uses perimeter garages as transfer nodes or gateways into the campus.

The building is organized around a linear, two-story, skylit circulation and exhibition courtyard. It is defined by an open stair and elevator tower at the entry, and by a grandstand stair at the student lounge/lecture theater end. The courtyard entry terminates a major campus circulation axis and admits passage to the multi-use exhibition gallery, a 200-seat lecture theater, and administrative offices. Seminar rooms and faculty offices flank the exhibition court, and parallel studios and shops that line the exterior facades.

The detail, use of materials, and expression of construction technologies reinforce the building's function as a learning and teaching laboratory for the study of architecture.

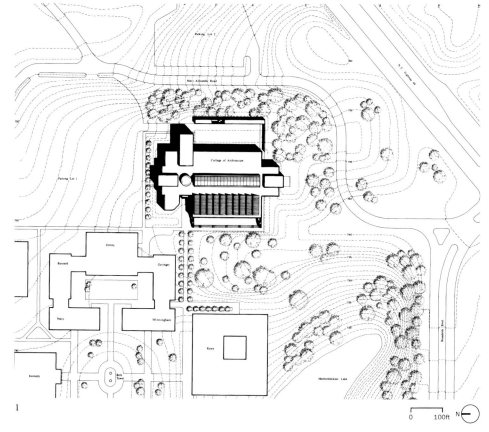

1

0   100ft   N

2

1　Site plan
2　Entry courtyard
3　View of building from northwest corner
4　Southwest facade from pedestrian walk

3

4

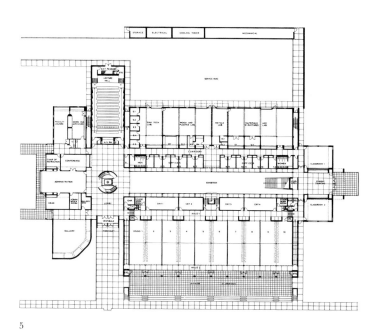

5

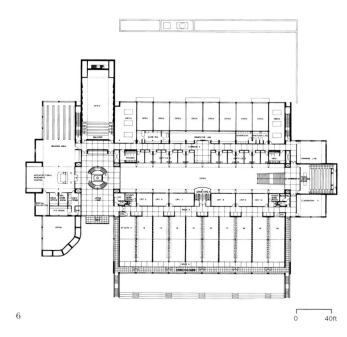

6

0   40ft

7

8

9

10

11

International Design Centers I & II

Design/Completion 1985/1987
Long Island City, New York
Lazard Development Corporation
1,000,000 square feet
Concrete frame, brick walls
Kalwall panels, skylights, steel pipe, trussed catwalks,
adjustable lighting

The International Design Center is a complex of four typical reinforced-concrete loft buildings of World War I vintage. Buildings I and II were renovated into design centers for the furniture and textile industries.

Center II was a seven-story building with an open courtyard. A trussed bridge at the open end of the plan provided the opportunity to create two major spaces: a skylit interior courtyard and an open entry court with an elevator core and lobby. A new catwalk beam for exterior lighting and display unifies the entry facade and acts as a gateway to the complex.

A decorative stair was added at the north end of the Center II atrium. Four new steel bridges span the atrium at the fourth floor level, vertically articulating the space and forming an implied second ceiling. A translucent skylight transforms the once open courtyard into a public room that orients the continuous open-balcony galleries adjoining the showroom spaces on each floor.

Center I, completed after Center II, is a horizontal five-story building organized along the same principles. The courtyard was enclosed to create a central atrium surrounded by showrooms. A cascading double stair was added to one side of the space, connecting all balcony levels with a central exposed elevator bridge. The Center I building is entered from a recessed arcade facing the Center II parking plaza, or from a ramped connecting bridge at levels three, four, and five. Spanning the street with its red metal and oculus fenestration, the 80-foot bridge is the project's graphic symbol.

1

2

1 Aerial view looking towards Manhattan
2 Center I and bridge detail
3 Section through Center II and Center I
4 Detail of facade entry
5 Bridge from Center II to Center I

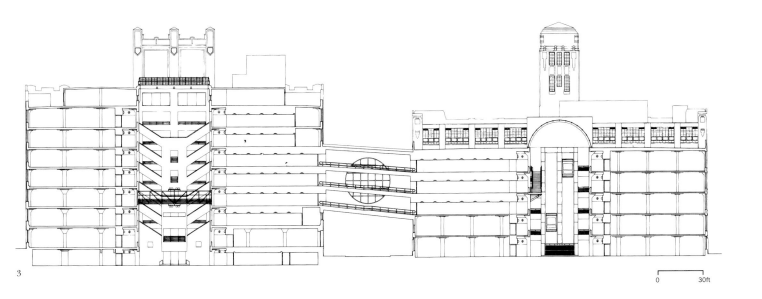

3

0   30ft

4

5

6　Center IV plan
7　Center III plan
8　Center II plan
9　Center I plan
10　Centers II and I from plaza
Opposite:
　　Center II atrium

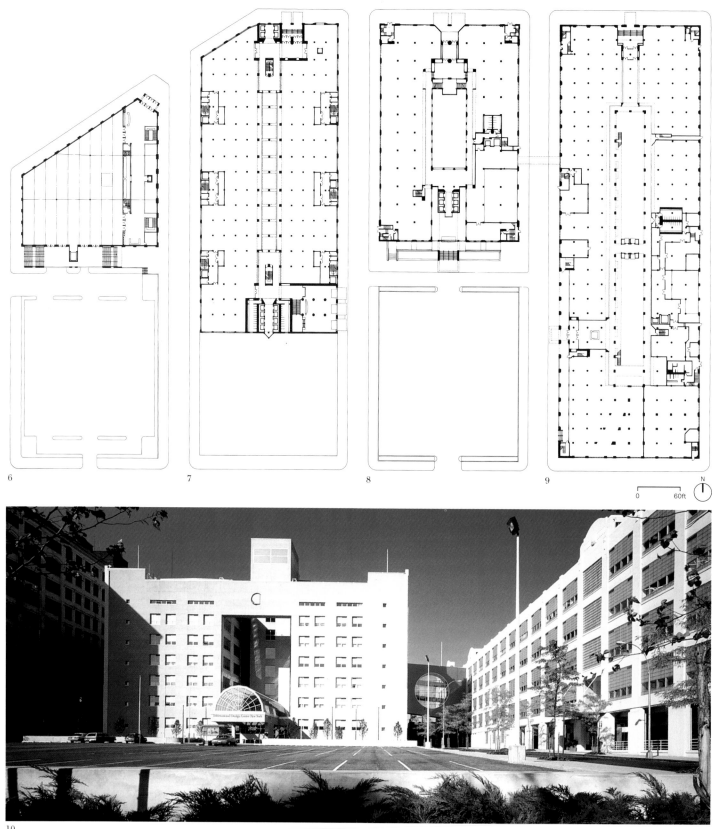

6

7

8

9

0　　　　　　60ft

N

10

12

14

15

13

16

17

Herman Miller Showroom, International Design Center

Design/Completion 1986/1987
Long Island City, New York
Herman Miller Inc.
21,000 square feet
Rubber flooring; carpet tiles; glass block; drywall; gridded opaque glass; acoustic tiles; custom painted millwork; etched glass; Formica cabinetwork; sandblasted concrete columns; fluorescent, incandescent and accent lighting

This showroom has a flexible design that allows for frequent reorganization of the space and changes of the displays while maintaining a constant sense of presence.

The 21,000-square-foot loft space is on the second floor of Center I in the International Design Center. The showroom is 13 feet 6 inches high with a raised mezzanine floor along its southern edge. Three-foot-diameter concrete columns frame the loft space at 20-foot intervals.

In addition to the display areas, the showroom contains a 60-seat multi-use audiovisual meeting space, a conference room, a pantry, a manager's office, staff workstations, and extensive storage space.

A custom-designed lighting grid defines the principal showroom areas. Suspended from the existing ceiling, the 10-foot-square grid establishes a second horizontal plane for accent lighting, display panels, and hanging fabric.

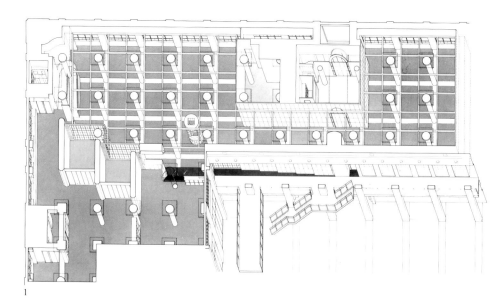

1

2

3

4

1 Axonometric
2 Kiosk and reception
3 View of ramp from second level
4 Detail of second level from stair
5 Entry from public balcony

5

6

7

8

9

Stevenson Hall, Oberlin College

Design/Completion 1986/1990
Oberlin, Ohio
Oberlin College
48,000 square feet
Amber and beige striped brick, aluminum window frames and doors,
porcelain panels

The building is organized to reinforce the intimate scale of the Oberlin campus and to support the residential house model of the college.

The site is adjacent to both institutional buildings and typical three-story Oberlin porch houses. The building massing reconciles these divergent surroundings by reinterpreting the porch house prototype into an institutional model.

Articulated by three identical, pyramidal, skylit dining halls on the second level, the new facility serves 800 students and faculty staff. A continuous linear element unites the three volumes, providing outdoor dining terraces on the upper level and a street-front porch on the lower level. An entry plaza offers access to the house entries, lounges, and administrative offices. This inverted organization provides natural light from above in what is a typically gray climate zone. It also allows three separate dining halls with a common servery and kitchen to be organized within one structure.

On the exterior, two colors of horizontally banded brick and cast stone relate to nearby buildings by Cass Gilbert. By reversing Gilbert's choice of materials, primarily limestone with brick trim, the building responds to the adjacent contextual fabric while establishing a dual-scaled hierarchical rendering for the new facility.

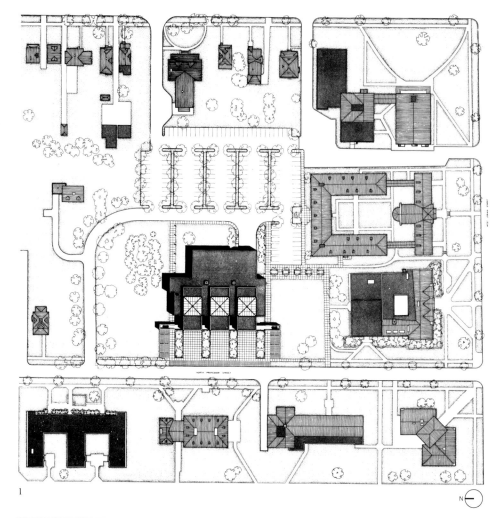

1

N

2

78

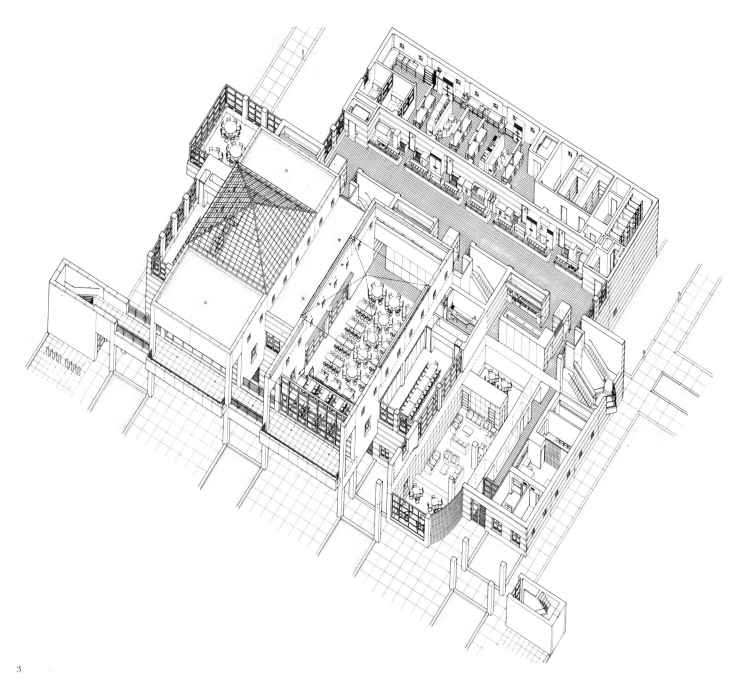

3

4

5

1 Site plan
2 West facade from campus
3 Axonometric
4 Pedestrian walk with entry porch and terrace above
5 Corner of south facade

6　Second floor plan
7　Ground floor plan
8　South interior stair
9　Servery with dining hall beyond
10　Typical student lounge space
Opposite:
　Typical dining hall

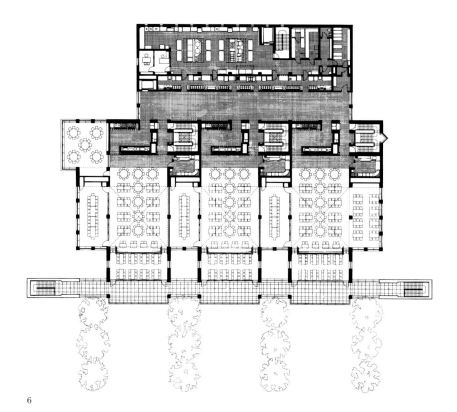

6

8

9

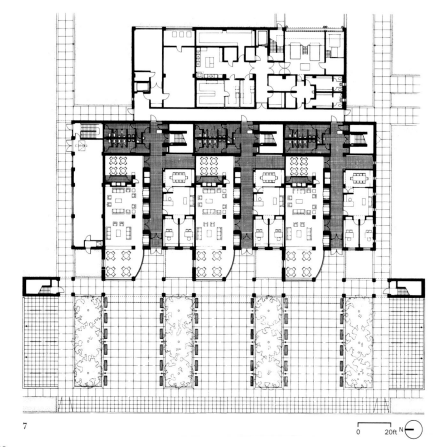

7

0　　20ft　N

10

SBK Entertainment World Inc. Offices

Design/Completion 1987/1988
New York, New York
SBK Entertainment World Inc.
42,000 square feet
Marble, honed black granite, ebonized oak, glass block, brass

This interior for a record and music publishing company occupies two floors of a typical 1960s Manhattan office building.

The plan is organized around a two-story entry and reception area. At the reception the architectural grid, articulated by the stone floor and oak wall panels, is modulated to create a wide cylindrical stair, connecting the elevator lobbies and internal corridor/gallery spaces to the perimeter offices.

Solid, transparent, and translucent planes delineate hierarchical spaces along the circulation galleries. Partners' offices are designed as loft volumes with panoramic views.

1

2

1 Entry/reception space
2 Reception space from stair
3 Screening room
4 Typical secretary workstations and circulation corridor
5 Northwest interior corner

3

4

5

6

7

8

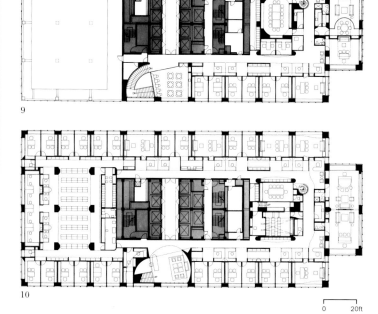

9

10

0   20ft

Oceanfront Residence

Design/Completion 1988/1992
Malibu, California
10,500 square feet
Private owner
Flamed buxy limestone, western cedar siding,
lead-coated copper standing seam roof
Maple veneered cabinets; aluminum windows and doors;
white, patterned, and clear glass

This private residence is located on a
16,500-square-foot site which parallels the
Pacific Coast Highway to the north and
the Pacific Ocean to the south. Two-story
residences define the east and west
boundaries. A combination of row house
and court house typologies generated the
parti. Interlocking building volumes and
outdoor spaces are layered within the
framework of the site, resulting in a
hierarchical sequence.

The highway facade is a layered, abstract
horizontal wall punctured by an entry gate
that leads to the first site layer. This wing
accommodates a screening room, a guest
house, and a garage on the ground floor,
and two children's bedrooms, a playroom,
and a caretaker's apartment (over the
garage) on the second floor.

The transition from the "gate house" to
the "main house" is through the second
layer pear tree courtyard. The courtyard
is defined to the east by a service wing,
accommodating the kitchen, pantry, and
breakfast room on the ground level, and
the exercise room, dressing room, and
master bathroom on the second level.
The courtyard is terminated to the west
by a bridge that connects the children's
suite to the main house.

The third layer establishes the main house
and provides a living room, dining room,
library, and porch on the ground level,
and the master bedroom, study, and decks
on the second level, all oriented towards
the ocean. The pool terrace extends the
pear tree courtyard west of the main house
and south of the gate house; it is in turn
extended to the south by the ocean
terrace to form the fourth site layer and
the edge to the beach.

The parti reinforces the visual and
psychological transition from the
acoustically invasive highway to the beach/
ocean horizon.

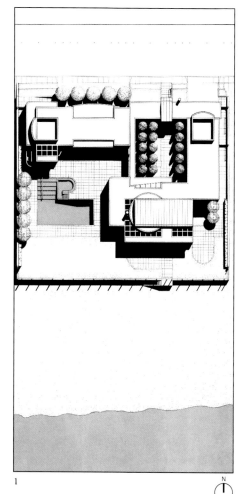

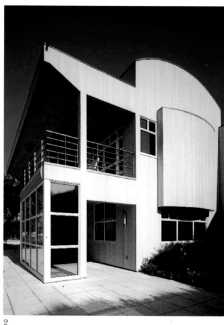

1 Site plan
2 Southeast corner of main house
3 View from southwest
4 North facade, closed to the road
5 South facade, open to the ocean

4

5

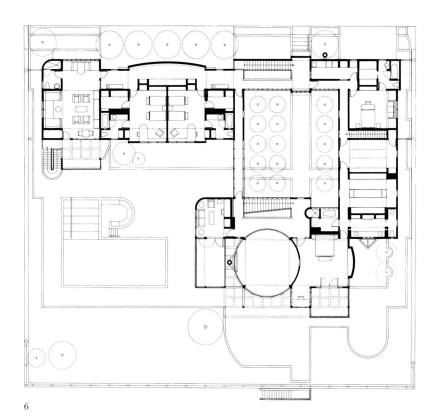

6

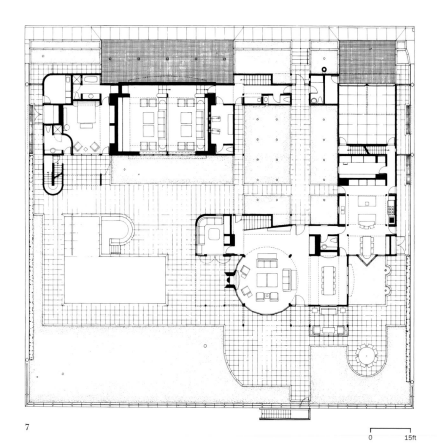

7

8

9

10

0   15ft

11

12

13

14

15

Werner Otto Hall, Busch-Reisinger Museum/ Fine Arts Library Addition to the Fogg Museum

Design/Completion 1988/1991
Cambridge, Massachusetts
Harvard University Art Museums
15,000 square feet
Indiana limestone, gray porcelain panels, glass block,
aluminum window and door frames, flamed granite

The task of designing a new building for the Busch-Reisinger Museum presented a challenging physical and theoretical problem. While the new building would be connected to a traditional structure, the Fogg Museum, it would also be adjacent to Le Corbusier's Modern masterpiece, the Carpenter Center, and would have to mediate this dual context. As with any urban infill development, it was necessary to address existing streetscape and scale relationships. The design also had to accommodate the constraints imposed by building above an existing underground library structure with limited load-bearing capacity. Finally, the client wanted the new building to have a presence and identity of its own, distinct from that of the Fogg Museum.

The program called for the building to house the new addition galleries and study archives for the Busch-Reisinger collection as well as parts of the Fine Arts Library relocated from the Fogg.

The solution refers to the formal architectural organization of the Fogg Museum design. One side of the existing atrium's perimeter circulation is extended into the new building and becomes the connection between the two major massing elements of the design. To the north are the primary spaces: the library reading room on the ground floor and the permanent collection galleries on the second floor. These are organized in a two-story element which extends the central axis of the Fogg to Prescott Street, presenting the new building's primary facade.

Continued

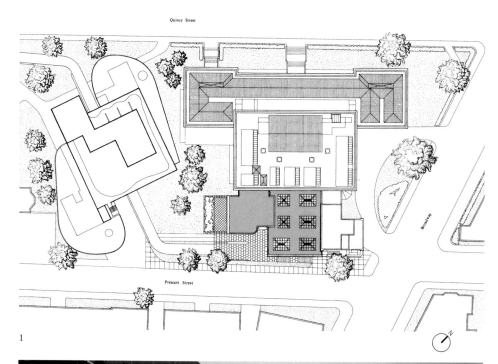

1

2

1   Site plan
2   East entry facade from street
3   East facade from the corner of Prescott Street and Broadway
4   Overall view showing completion/extension of Carpenter Center ramp
     through site
5   Detail of south facade
6   South facade from Carpenter Center

3

4

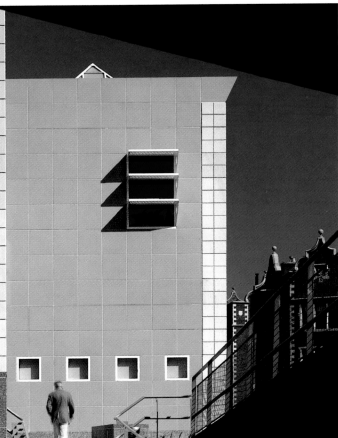

5

6

To the south are the support and smaller spaces: the library staff offices on the ground floor, the temporary exhibition gallery on the second floor, and the study archives on the third floor. These spaces are organized in a three-story element which is set back from the street and rotated 90 degrees to address the Carpenter Center. The interlocked massing of these two elements completes the orthogonal building framework which surrounds the Carpenter Center.

The solution also resolves Le Corbusier's compelling site circulation idea. The Carpenter Center ramp, which was intended to provide a mid-block public walkway from Quincy Street to Prescott Street through the building, ended in the Fogg's rear yard without a connection to the sidewalk. The design extends the ramp onto a new plaza from which one can either enter the library or descend a new exterior stair to the street.

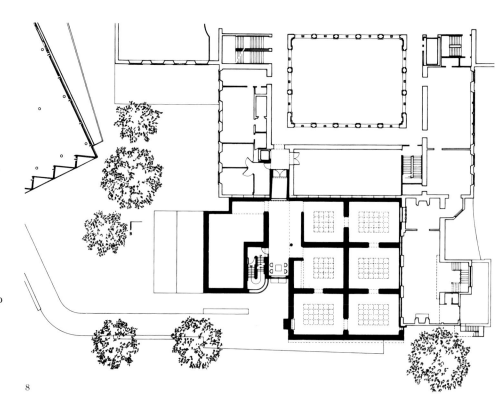

8

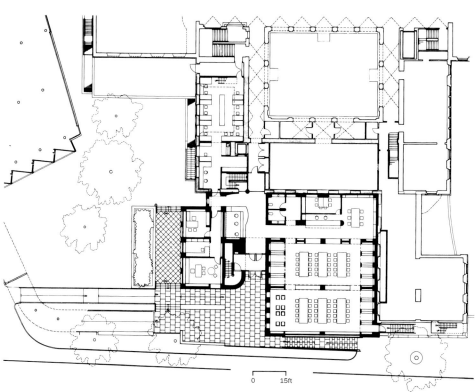

0   15ft

7

9

92

7   South window from gallery
8   Second floor plan
9   Ground floor plan
10 Entry gallery
11 Study archives
12 Permanent collection galleries
13 Study archives detail

10

11

12

13

14 North section
15 South section
16 Section
Opposite:
   Permanent collection galleries

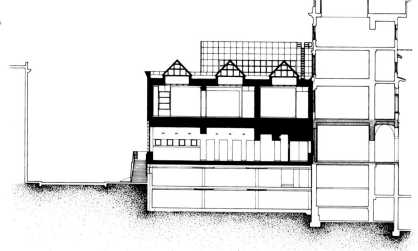

14

15

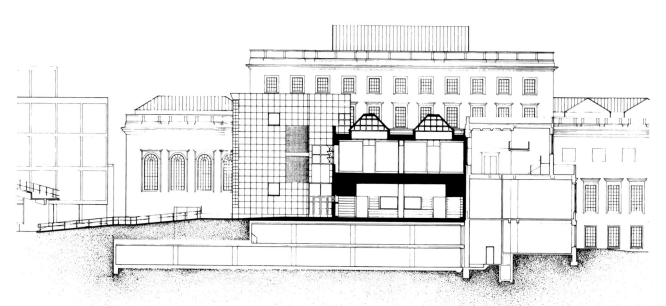

16

Gwathmey Apartment

Design/Completion 1988/1991
New York, New York
Charles Gwathmey
2,500 square feet
Maple and travertine floors, plaster walls and ceilings,
lacquered cabinetwork and millwork

The Gwathmey Apartment transforms a typical 2,500-square-foot Fifth Avenue apartment into a spatially complex pavilion loft with a design that represents and summarizes ideas and provokes further investigations.

A balance between stable and dynamic spaces is expressed by asymmetrical plan manipulations that provide a counterpoint to the existing exterior window walls while recentering the interior facades. The space appears carved rather than assembled, juxtaposing a sense of weight and density with the openness of the plan.

Objects of art, collected over time, allude to historical design preferences and serve as reference points in the object–space dynamic of the parti. Materials reinforce the program and the volume manipulations, adding to the sense of collage while supporting the hierarchy of articulated details.

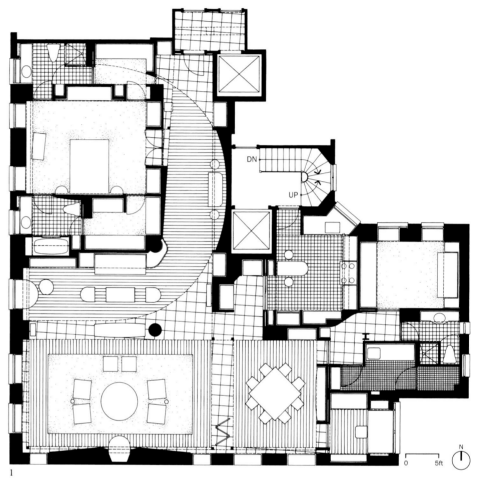

1

1   Floor plan
2   Sitting/living room
Opposite:
    Entrance gallery from living room

2

4 Master bedroom
5 Master bathroom
6 Gallery from entry
7 Fireplace wall detail
Opposite:
  Dining area

4

5

6

7

Universal Studios Inc. Divisional Headquarters

Design/Completion 1989/1998
Beverly Hills, California
Universal Studios Inc.
90,000 square feet (office building);
130,000 square feet (below-grade garage)
Granite base with limestone walls, beech wood, stainless steel,
reinzink (zinc) panels, Kalcurve

This project is located in the Beverly Hills Industrial District where zoning restrictions limit the height of buildings to three stories. The typical cornice line along Third Street is reinterpreted by a barrel-vaulted, translucent Kalcurve skylight running the length of the building and incorporating the third-floor executive offices.

Site and program variants are exploited to create a complex, hierarchically asymmetrical building. The screening room marks the garage entry and ramp; conference rooms occupy a tower at the corner, adjoining a plaza and a reflecting pool and fountain. The four-story conical atrium is the central volume in the building, accommodating entry, reception, and vertical circulation.

The primary rectilinear mass is clad with a combination of smooth gray limestone and textured green granite in contrast to the zinc panels of the screening room, conference tower, and elevator core. The industrial steel window system has a powder-coated finish and is glazed with gray tinted and ceramic frit glass. Entrance railings and miscellaneous trim are in stainless steel.

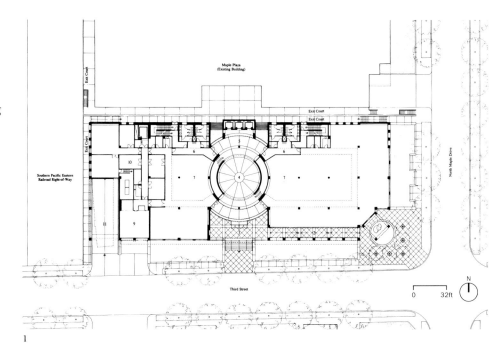

1

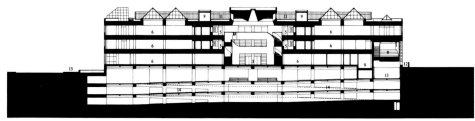

2

3

1 Ground floor plan
2 Longitudinal section
3 View of building at the intersection of Third Street and West Maple Drive
4 Entry circulation rotunda
5 Southwest corner from Third Street

4

5

Contemporary Resort Convention Center, Walt Disney World

Design/Completion 1989/1991
Lake Buena Vista, Florida
Walt Disney Corporation
120,000 square feet
Painted stucco, enameled steel panels, glass block, aluminum window system
Painted gypsum board, stained oak, fabric panels, custom metal ceiling, custom painted carpet

The Contemporary Resort Convention Center is an addition to Walt Disney's visionary Contemporary Hotel, completed in 1971. A new 2.5-acre entry plaza joins the two buildings and leads to a porte-cochere entry for the hotel. The addition accommodates a 45,000-square-foot conference room that can be divided into three multipurpose spaces; a 7,000-square-foot ballroom; three prefunction spaces; five meeting rooms; and a full-service kitchen with loading facilities.

Situated at the center of the parti, the main ballroom is flanked by meeting rooms at either end. The entry and prefunction spaces are layered across the front of the building, with the kitchen and support areas located at the rear. Natural light, color, and texture mark the primary and secondary circulation systems and articulate the major volumes. The building's horizontal silhouette is reinforced by the strong use of color, which contrasts with the vertical, gridded facade of the hotel.

Four major elements create a collage/assemblage: the curved, striped primary volume of the main ballroom and prefunction gallery; the entry canopy and skylit porte-cochere; and the two rotundas, one connected to the hotel by stairs, escalators, and a glass-block bridge, and the other accented by a square punched window which presents an iconic form on the more visible west corner.

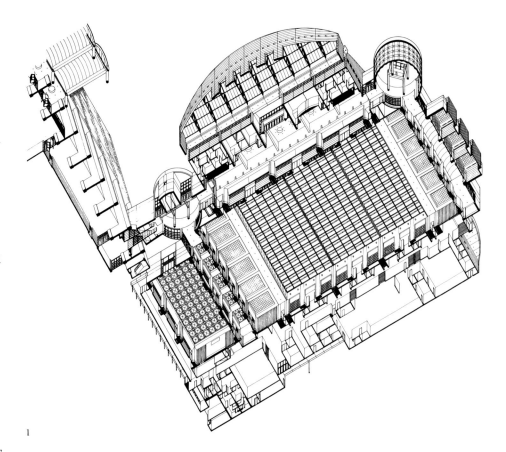

1

2

1   Axonometric view from below
2   Overall view from Lake Buena Vista
3   Overall view from Lake Buena Vista by night
4   North facade
5   Entry plaza and vehicular entry arcade

3

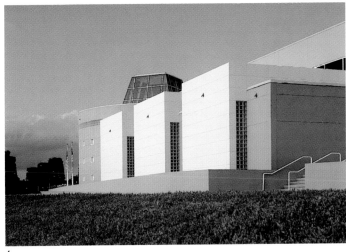

4

5

6   Interior of north rotunda
7   Main prefunction space
8   Main ballroom

6

7

8

Zumikon Residence

Design/Completion 1990/1992
Zumikon, Switzerland
Thomas and Christina Bechtler
10,225 square feet
Concrete base; white stucco walls; green limestone accent walls;
stainless steel handrails; standing seam, terne-coated stainless steel
roofs; gray sandstone and steamed beech flooring and cabinetry

This private residence is located on a site near Zurich, offering panoramic views towards Lake Zurich and the Alps. Zoning laws required a strict relationship between the topography of the hillside and the height of the building.

The formal elements of the structure are organized as a cluster of interconnected parts whose overlapping fragments evoke images of a dense rural village built up over time. The Z-shaped plan creates two outdoor spaces: a main terrace which, like the village square, acts as a referential outdoor room, and a three-level roof terrace, perceived from the exterior as a natural sloping green courtyard.

The spatial organization of the house is defined by a north–south circulation spine, accommodating an art gallery and a dining room, with the remaining public and living areas grouped at either end.

Continued

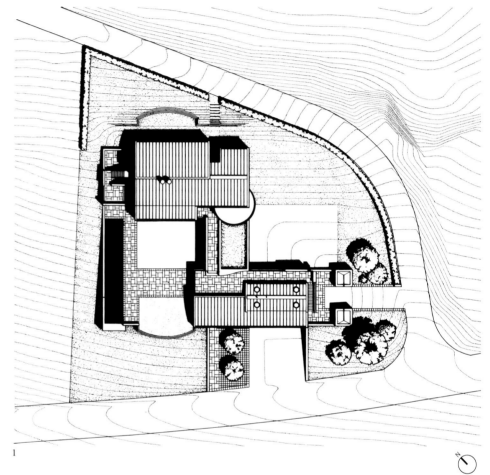

1

2

1 Site plan
2 South facade
3 South terrace detail
4 South facade detail
5 South facade and terrace

3

4

5

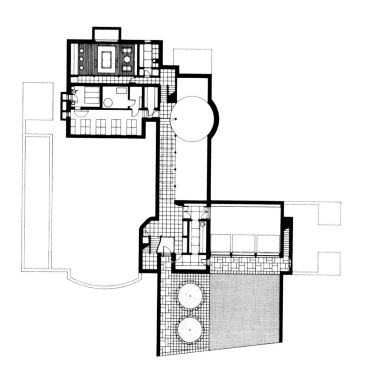

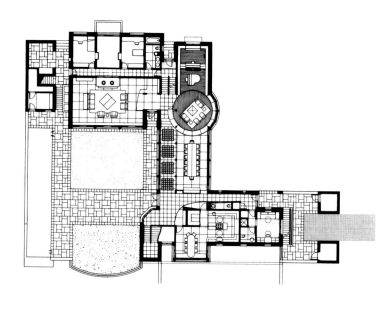

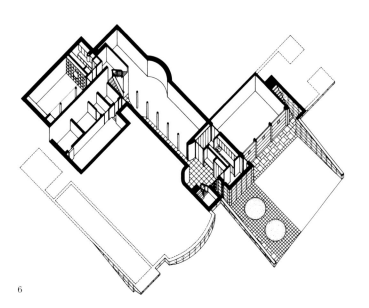

6

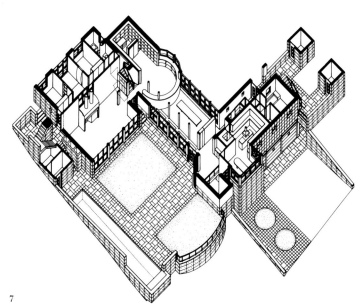

7

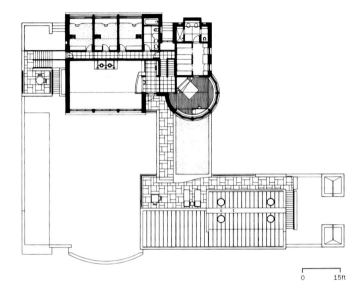

Private spaces are situated above and behind public areas, with the master bedroom set in the cylinder above the library, and the children's bedrooms and playrooms occupying three levels behind and above the living room. The division of public and private space provides privacy while integrating communal areas for family interaction.

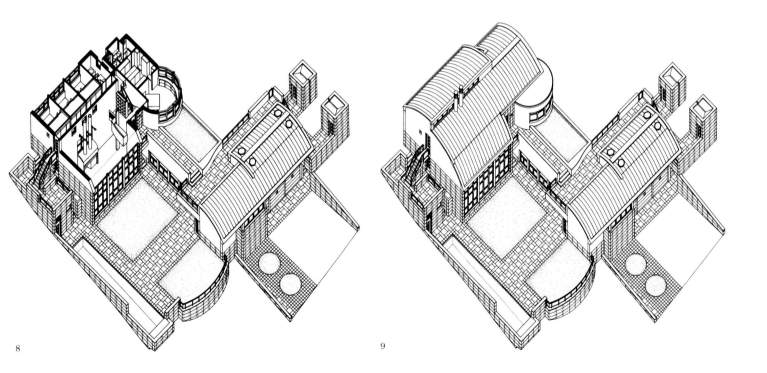

8

9

10

11

12

13

14

15

16

Taipei Residence

Design 1990
Taipei, Taiwan
Private owner
40,000 square feet

This private residence is located on a 10,000-square-foot sloping suburban site, enclosed by a volcanic wall and restricted by vertical and horizontal zoning regulations. The design solution was derived from the program, the site restrictions, and the Chinese cultural tradition of separating private and public spaces.

The public entry leads to a four-and-a-half-story gallery that visually extends the garden below grade with a two-story south-facing glass wall and grand stair. The private entry overlooks the gallery and public entry from a balcony on the north side. It leads to the stair and elevator core, and to a ramp-bridge across the gallery that connects with guest units on the intermediate half-level.

The 11,000-square-foot private domain reaches five stories above grade and creates a visual "object" in the garden. On the second floor are the children's and grandparent's bedrooms, a music room, playrooms, and lounge areas. The third floor provides a two-story living room and dining room, a kitchen, and a *teppanyaki* (game) room. The fourth floor houses the master bedroom, a study, and a Jacuzzi terrace with access to the private garden via an outdoor stair.

The 30,000-square-foot public domain is located on the two lower levels and is accessed from the grand stairs. Facilities include a ballroom and theater space, a game room, a bar and wine cellar, a full-service kitchen and ancillary service spaces, a squash court and spa, and a six-car garage. Service and mechanical spaces are located on the two basement mezzanine levels. All are accessed and interconnected by the service elevator and stairs.

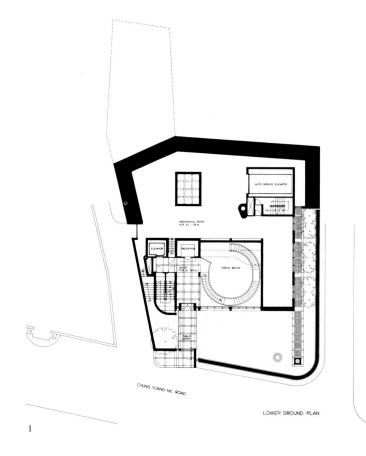

LOWER GROUND PLAN

1

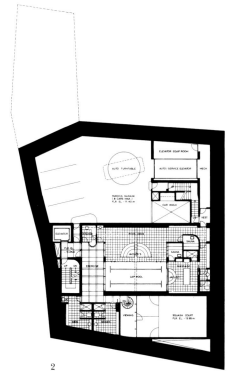

2

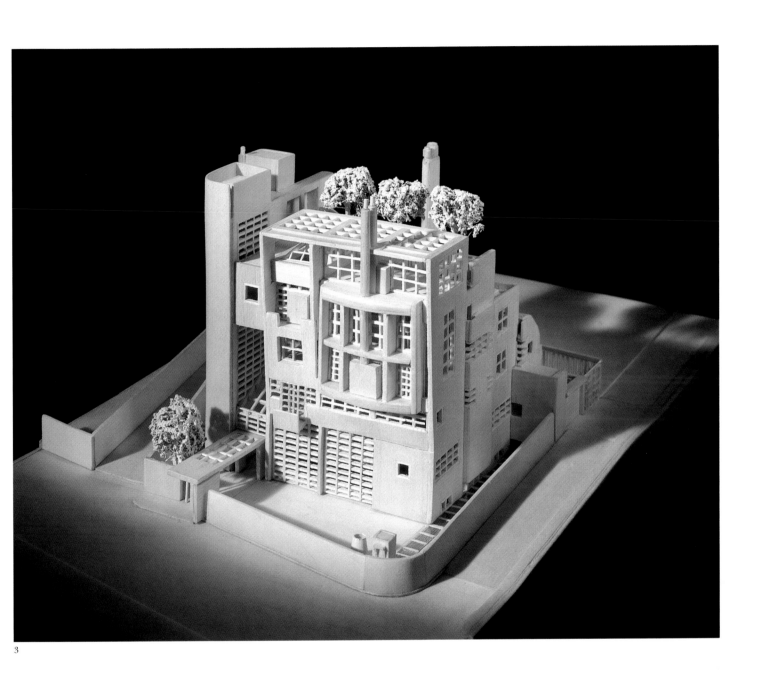

3

1   Public entry ground floor plan
2   Lower level basement plan
3   South facade

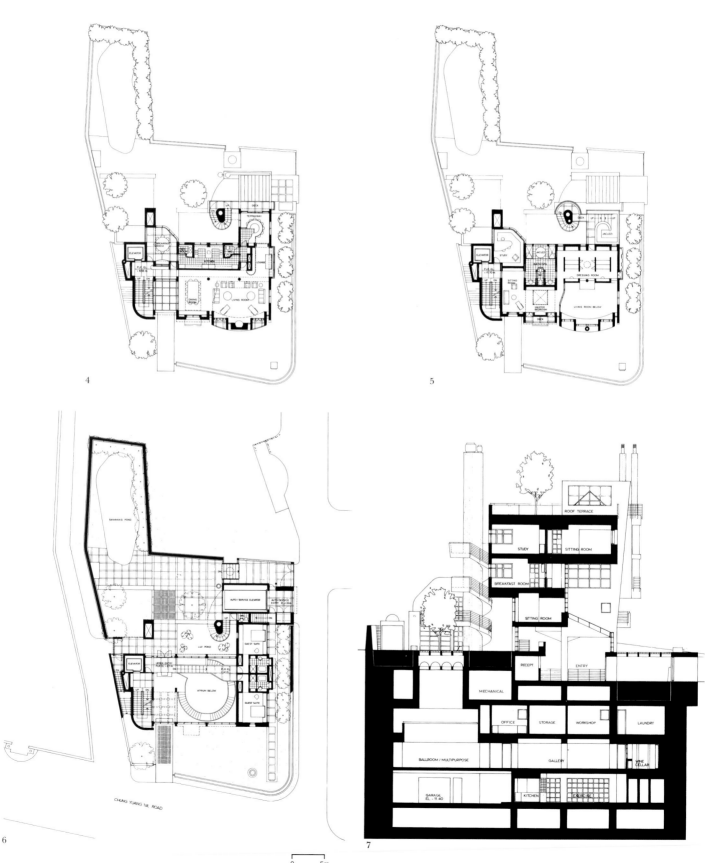

4

5

6

CHUNG YUANG 1st ROAD

7

0   5m

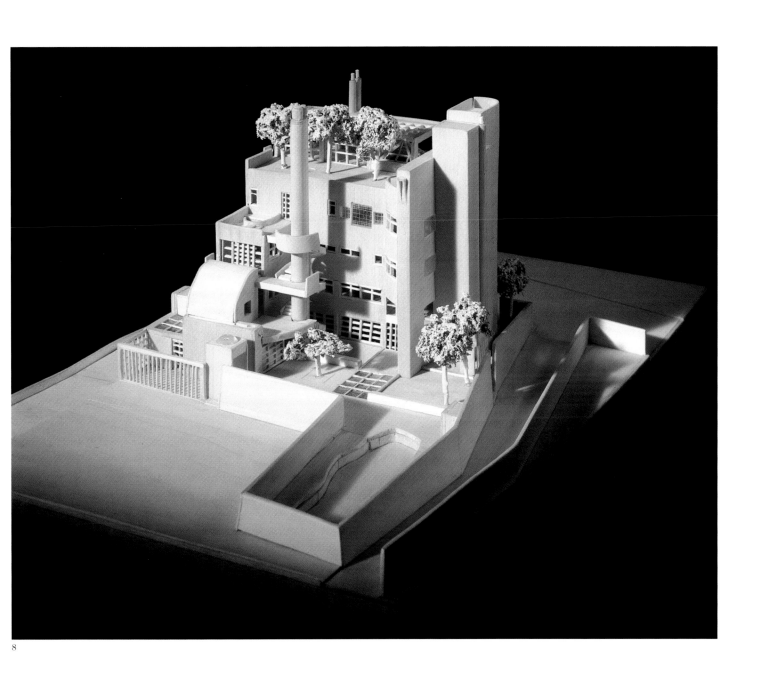

8

Ronald S. Lauder Foundation Offices

Design/Completion 1990/1992
New York, New York
Ronald S. Lauder Foundation
10,000 square feet
Ebonized cherry, millwork, cherry wood and marble floors,
painted canvas and plaster walls

The Ronald S. Lauder Foundation is
located on the 42nd floor of a building
overlooking Central Park. The offices
occupy a narrow, rectangular 10,000-
square-foot space organized by a single
circulation spine/gallery.

The reception/meeting space integrates
the circulation gallery with an adjacent
conference room. The spine ends in a
rotunda that marks the entrance to
Lauder's own office, library, dining room,
and private work space. A series of
secretarial workstations, backed by small
private offices, line the perimeter of the
spine; a small conference room and
service areas are located in the interior.

The proportions of the offices enhance
the sense of intimacy created by Lauder's
extensive furniture and art collection. The
architectural detailing suggests, without
imitating, the sense of texture and surface
articulation that were central to the craft
ethic of the Secessionist period.

1

1 Entry/waiting space
2 Typical workstations
3 Floor plan
4 Main conference room

2

116

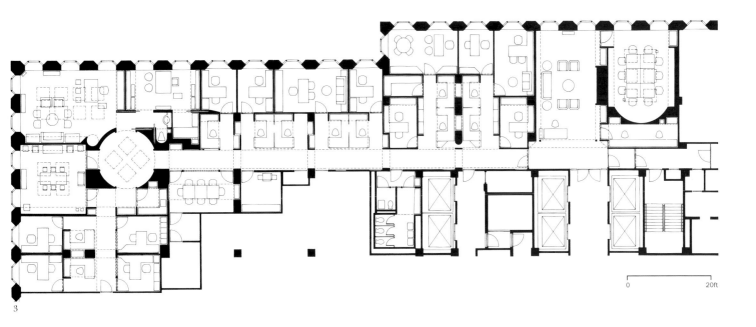

3

4

5 Rotunda
6 Private dining room
Opposite:
 Exhibition gallery

5

6

Capital Group Inc. Offices

Design/Completion 1991/1993
West Los Angeles, California
Capital Group Inc.
32,000 square feet
Maple cabinets, doors and frames; wall covering; plastic laminate;
gypsum drywall; vinyl flooring; linear metal ceilings; ceiling tiles;
glass block

The team-oriented approach of this investment group is reflected in the egalitarian, non-hierarchical environment of their West Los Angeles offices. There are no corner offices; instead, conference rooms, a boardroom, library, and staff lounge occupy the corners of the two 16,000-square-foot floor plates, with the individual offices and group workstations between them at the perimeter.

A two-story entry and reception space is articulated by an open stair leading to a glass-block bridge that connects with circulation galleries filled with contemporary art. Natural light penetrates the galleries from interior clerestory windows in the office walls.

Each office module has a conference table to facilitate discussions and a U-shaped counter that provides a generous horizontal work surface for an ever-changing assortment of office machines. The perimeter offices were designed to maximize efficiency and flexibility, both technologically and spatially. An integrated cabinet and millwork system of wood paneling and translucent and transparent glass establishes the aesthetic of the entire space.

The company's "open door" philosophy created special acoustic requirements. Recessed doorways to individual offices are lined with perforated vinyl to reduce sound transmission. Ceiling and floor finishes provide additional noise control, and, like the corridor elevations, reflect the functions of different spaces.

1

2

1 Entry/reception space
2 Typical corner of public corridor
3 Second level entry bridge

3

4 15th floor plan
5 16th floor plan
6 Conference room/waiting reception
7 Secretary workstations
8 Associate's office
9 Main conference room

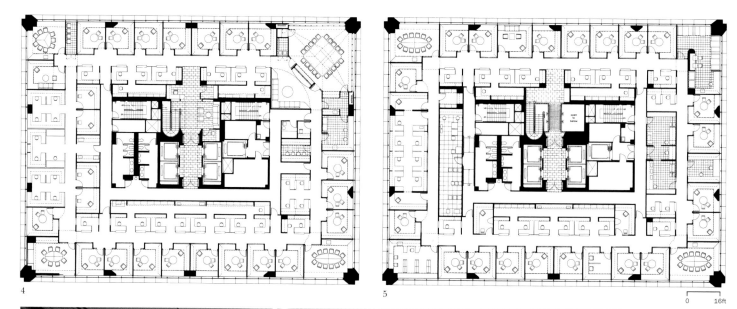

4

5

0   16ft

6

122

7

8

9

PepsiCo Headquarters Dining Facilities

Design/Completion 1995/1996
Purchase, New York
PepsiCo Inc.
18,000 square feet
Steamed Danish beech, marble, brushed stainless steel,
acrylic panels, plaster barrel vaults, Almute

This project is the first phase of an ongoing Gwathmey Siegel master plan for the extensive PepsiCo headquarters. Situated in a suburb of New York City, the complex was originally designed by Edward Durrell Stone in the late 1960s. The program includes food preparation areas, storage and mechanical rooms, a self-service cafeteria, and dining room and garden areas.

The entry lobby joins two circulation nodes and displays a "logo wall" of back-lit acrylic panels inflected towards the cafeteria entrance. Inside the cafeteria, food serveries and counter walls are distributed at the perimeter of the space to allow maximum flexibility for equipment arrangements, as well as uninterrupted circulation into the dining area. The main dining room seats up to 300 people and provides access to the patio and garden beyond.

The overall 5-foot planning grid of the PepsiCo complex was used to develop a proportioning system that locates and unifies all architectural, electrical, and mechanical elements.

2

1

3

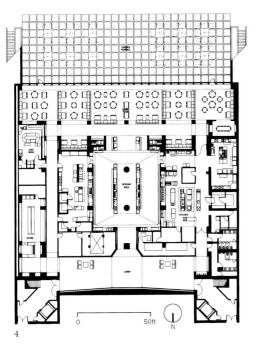

1   Dining room detail
2   Entrance lobby
3   Servery
4   Floor plan
5   Dining space

4

5

Social Sciences Building and Computer Center, University of California at San Diego

Design/Completion 1991/1995
La Jolla, California
University of California at San Diego
75,000 square feet
Exposed concrete, black and white ceramic tiles, stucco, powder-coated aluminum panels, brushed stainless steel, frosted glass, reflective glass

This facility is situated at the top of a ridge affording panoramic views of the Pacific Ocean to the west and the mountains to the east; it runs parallel to Ridgewalk, the major north–south pedestrian spine of the campus.

The ground floor accommodates conference seminar rooms, laboratories, a media room, and demonstration classrooms situated adjacent to a series of open courtyards which provide space for informal public gatherings. The second through fourth floors contain the administration and faculty offices for six departments within the Social Sciences division: Latin American Studies, Sociology, Urban Studies, Political Science, Anthropology, and Ethnic Studies.

The exterior is clad in a combination of white and black ceramic tiles and light gray stucco, with accent walls and columns in powder-coated aluminum panels. Railings and miscellaneous metal trim are in brushed stainless steel. The operable window system combines jalousies with integral louvers, frosted glass clerestories, and reflective glass view windows, forming a composite environmental wall system. Ceiling fans and operable transoms over the doors provide cross-ventilation.

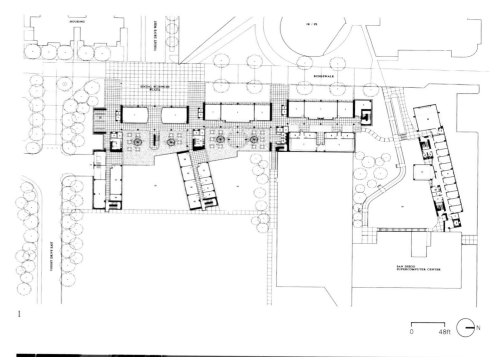

1

0   48ft

2

3

4

1 Site/ground floor plan
2 View from the southwest
3 View from the east
4 View from the southeast
5 View to demonstration room from supercomputer addition
6 Detail of east facade of supercomputer office addition
7 Detail of supercomputer office and entrance
8 View of supercomputer office addition

5

6

7

8

9   Third floor plan
10   Second floor plan
11   Typical office workstation
12   Corridor detail
13   Detail of entrance to supercomputer addition
Opposite:
   View from west of supercomputer office addition with demonstration room on the left

11

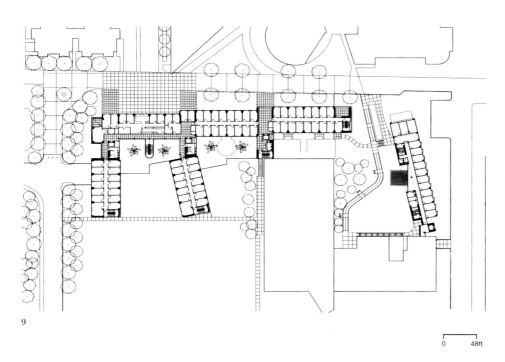
9

0   48ft

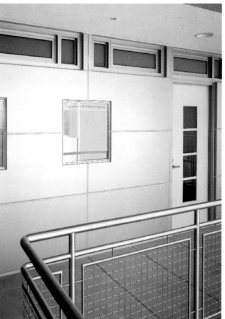
12

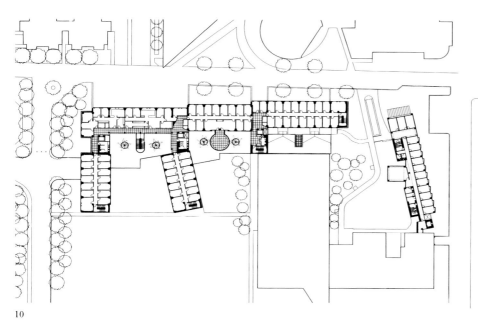
10

13

The Science, Industry and Business Library (SIBL),
New York Public Library

Design/Completion 1991/1996
New York, New York
The New York Public Library
25,000 square feet
Oak, stainless steel, terrazzo, solid and laminated black plastic, synthetic
plaster, acoustic plaster, painted gypsum board, carpet tiles

This 21st century, state-of-the-art library
is housed on five levels of the landmark
former B. Altman Building. The fully
retrofitted structure accommodates an
open shelf reference collection, periodical
shelving, catalog areas, reference
specialists supported by
a complete reference department, open
micro-form shelving, reading areas, an
electronic information center, a training
center, meeting rooms, a 1,300,000-
volume compact stacked space, and a full-
service circulating library. In addition to
the public spaces and reserve stacks, the
facility provides for 50,000 square feet of
library administration office space.

Continued

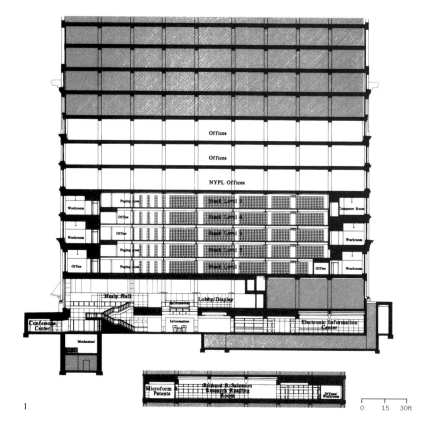

1

1   North–south section
2   Entry from Madison Avenue
Opposite:
    Elevator at main level

2

4

5

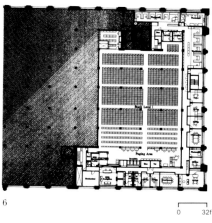

6

0   32ft

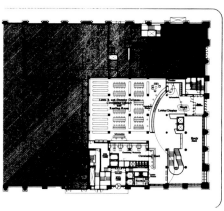

7

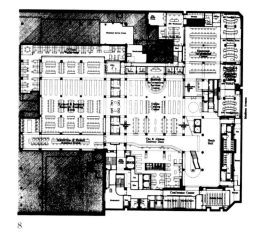

8

The public areas are distributed on the ground and lower levels, providing maximum horizontal adjacency for the research library on the lower level, and easy public access to the circulating library at entry level. The stacks and administration offices are situated on the upper levels, with staff areas surrounding the climate-controlled, structurally reinforced stack area.

9

10

11

12

13

11 Typical workstation detail
12 Research library entrance from Healy Hall
13 Lower level library
14 Research reading room, lower level library
15 Electronic information center

14

15

Stadtportalhäuser

Design 1991–1994
Frankfurt-am-Main, Germany
Bosch Corporation
2,000,000 square feet

This project is located at the intersection of a major boulevard leading into the city of Frankfurt, at the edge of the international exposition center. The design resolution was influenced both by the importance of maintaining the site trees and an open park space and by the existing railroad bridge, road system, and exposition structures.

The complex volumetric configurations were specific responses to the site and program, which included a museum and office building for the Bosch Corporation, two speculative office buildings, and a hotel. Essential to the composition are the two similar wedge-shaped office buildings whose facades define the gate, and the dissimilar masses that extend from these facades to either side of the boulevard.

The project was the first European competition for the Gwathmey Siegel office; the scale and complexity of the architectural and urban resolutions represent a creative learning experience and provide an excellent resource for future investigations.

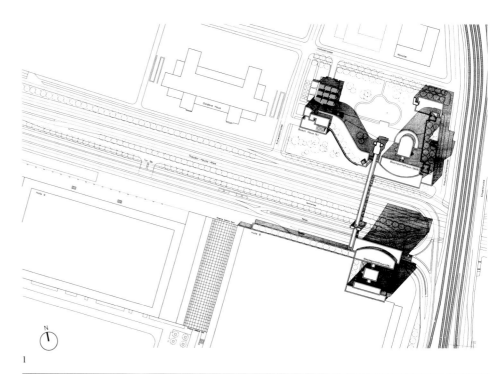

1

2

136

1 Site plan
2 Aerial view of model from north showing museum park, Bosch Corporation building, two speculative office buildings, and hotel
3 Design intention
4 Aerial view of model from south

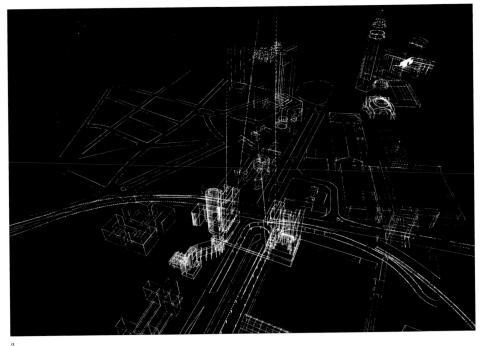

3

4

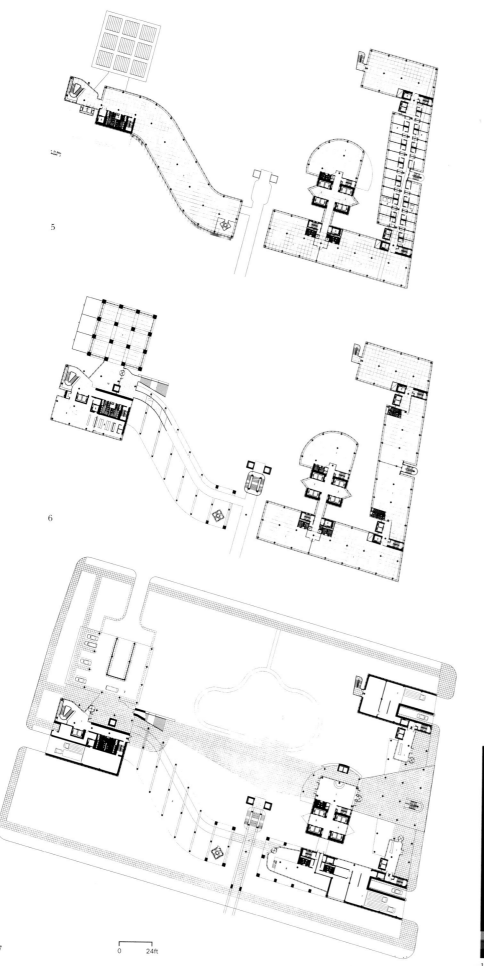

5

6

7

8

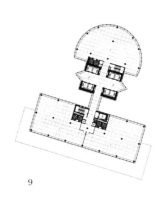

9

0   24ft

10

11

Master Plan and Three Academic Buildings, Pitzer College

Design/Completion 1991/1995
Claremont, California
Pitzer College
39,500 square feet
Painted stucco walls, painted standing seam steel roof,
painted aluminum doors and windows

The intent of the master plan was to site three new buildings to redefine the existing campus landscape plan, to define new outdoor spaces, and to establish a more compelling presence and sense of place for the campus.

The simultaneous design of the master plan, landscape plan, and buildings offered an efficient, integrated, composite strategy that transforms the original campus.

1

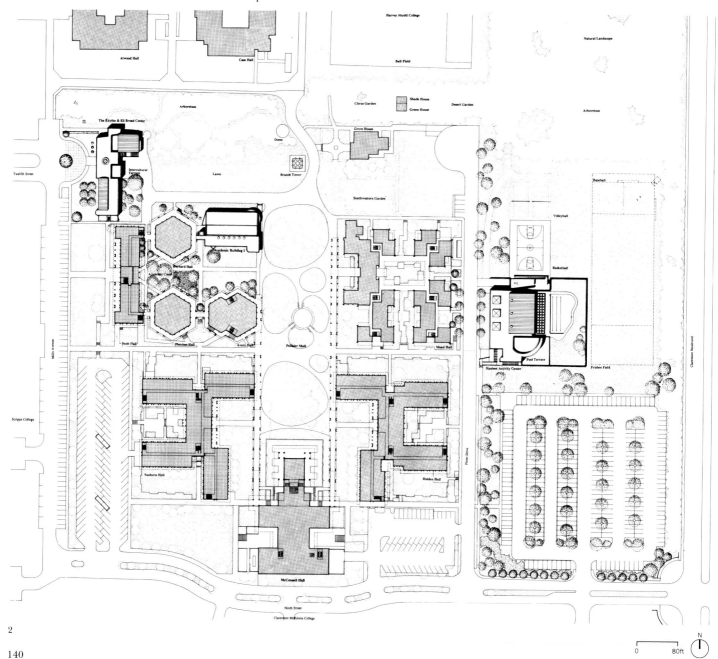

2

Edythe and Eli Broad Center

The 13,000-square-foot Edythe and Eli Broad Center creates a new entry/gateway to the campus. Located at the primary intersection, on axis with Brandt Tower, and framing the previously open-ended lawn, Broad Center becomes the initial architectural image and experience for visitors and students. The center accommodates an art gallery, a musical performance and lecture space, classrooms, seminar rooms, admission offices, faculty offices, and the President's office. The program is expressed by the building's geometric forms and the animated use of color. The two-story entry space is articulated by a glass-block ceiling and conical skylight, and acts as the public orientation space and entrance plaza to the campus.

3

4

5

1   Exterior view of Broad Hall and Edythe and Eli
    Broad Center
2   Master site plan
3   West facade public entry
4   Detail of public entry
5   View from lawn

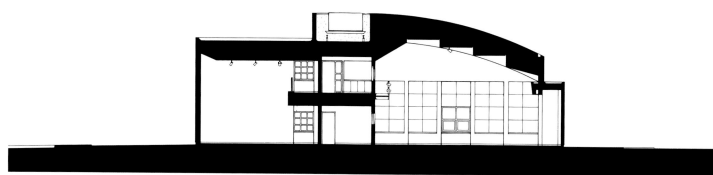

6

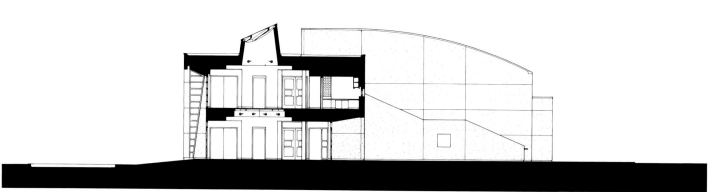

7

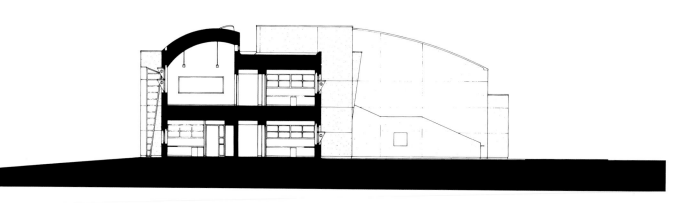

8

9

10

11   Ground floor lobby
Opposite:
    Second level reception

11

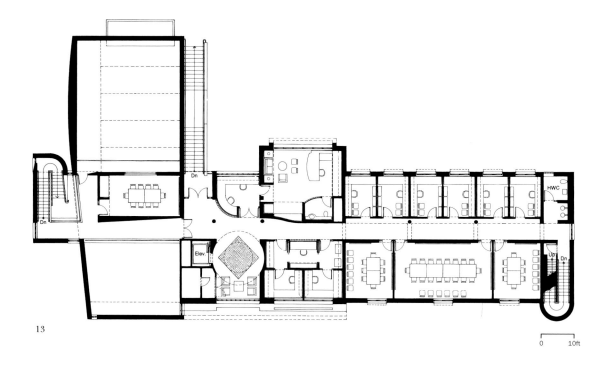

13

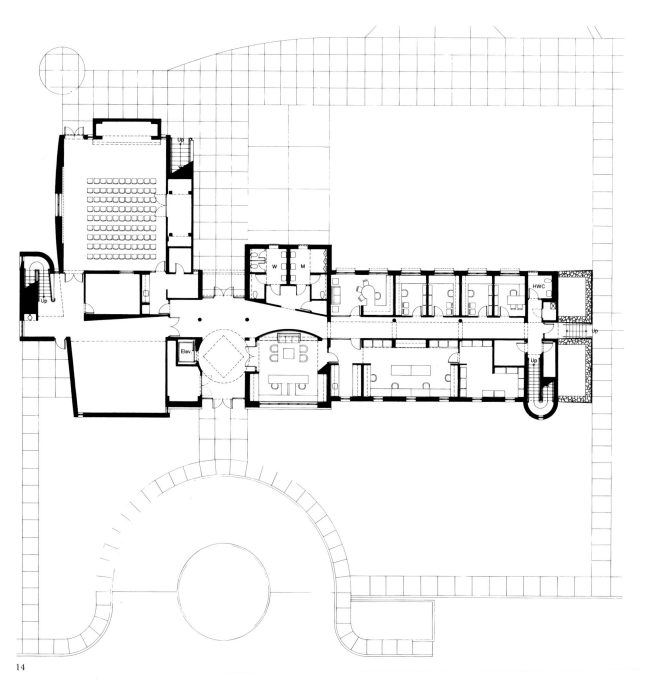

14

13 Second level plan
14 Ground level plan
15 Exhibition gallery
16 President's office

15

16

17 Typical classroom
18 Stairwell

17

Broad Hall Classroom Building

The 14,500-square-foot Broad Hall houses classrooms, faculty offices, a language center, a computer center, and psychology and anthropology laboratories. The building is sited to complete the previously undefined academic quadrangle, to reinforce the corner of Pellisier Mall, and to define, with Broad Center, the new Pitzer Lawn. This contextual intervention integrates architecture with landscape design, enriching and ordering disparate existing conditions as well as establishing a dynamic new sense of place.

19

19 View from existing building to campus green
20 Bridge to new building
21 Broad Hall from campus
22 Campus green facade

20

21

22

Master Plan and Three Academic Buildings, Pitzer College 151

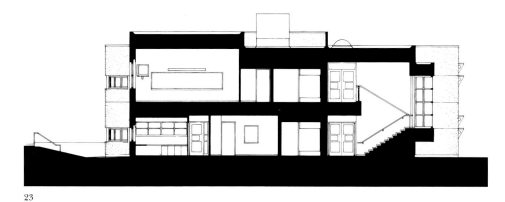

23

26

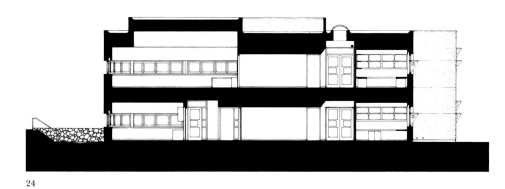

24

27

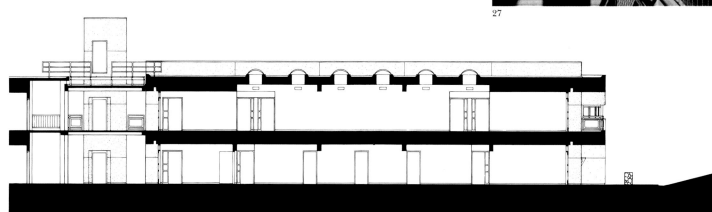

25

28

0   10ft

29

30

31

32

The third building is the Gold Student Activity Center, a 12,000-square-foot two-story structure which establishes a second major outdoor cross-axis on the campus. The program includes a new snack bar and pool/garden terrace, as well as a subdividable assembly space, student offices, a post office, lounges, lockers, and a two-story active recreation room.

30   Facade detail
31   Exterior view
32   View of entry facade
33   Longitudinal section AA
34   Lateral section BB
35   Lateral section CC

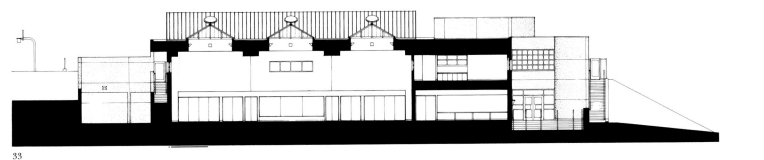

33

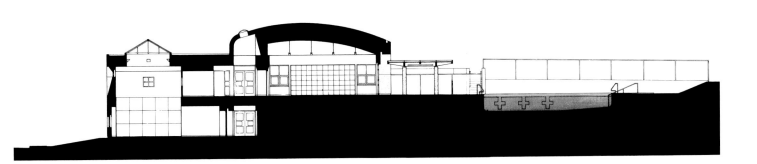

34

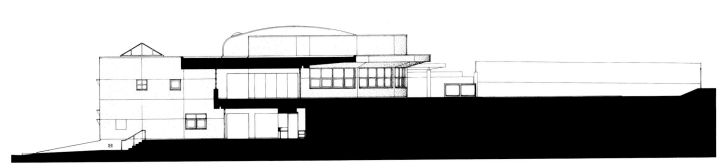

35

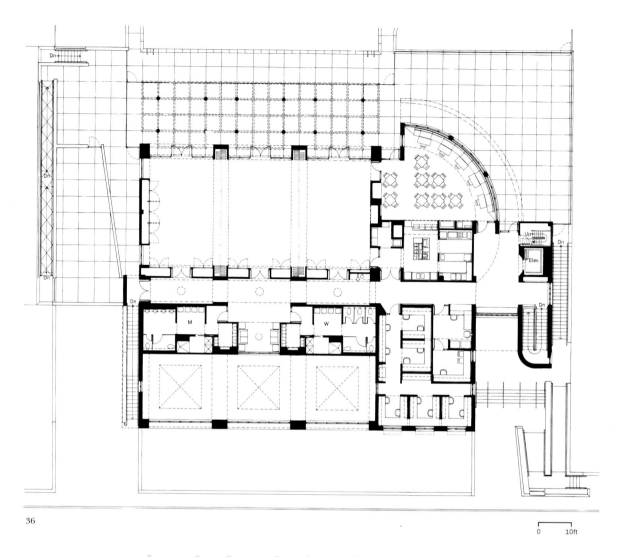

36

0   10ft

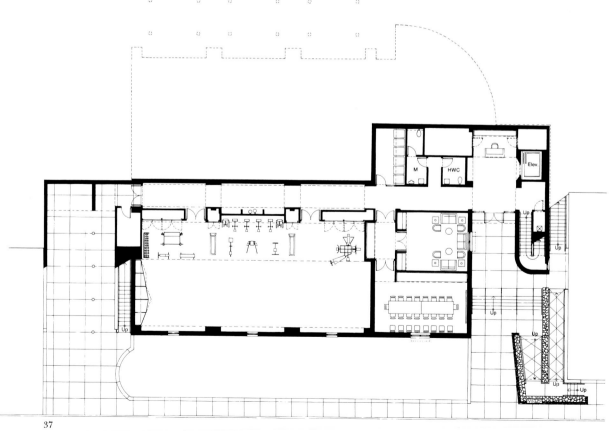

37

36 Second level plan
37 Ground level plan
38 Second floor gallery
39 Flexible exercise space
40 Snack bar

38

39

40

Convention Center and Hotel, EuroDisney

Design 1989–1991
Marne-la-Vallée, France
EuroDisney, SCA
120,000 square feet

The proposed convention center and hotel is the largest single building project at EuroDisney to date. The design accommodates a 750-room convention hotel with restaurants, meeting facilities, and health spa, and direct access to a 300,000-square-foot multidimensional convention center with a 2,000-seat industrial theater, an exhibition pavilion, ballrooms, a lecture theater, meeting rooms, and full food service facilities.

The project is located at the entrance to the EuroDisney complex and rejects the "decorated box" theme of the surrounding hotels. The new building instead reads as a collection of forms, silhouettes, and facades expressing the relationship between exterior form and interior volume.

The sequential ordering and integration of exterior spaces, transitions, and circulation organizes the interior and articulates a constantly varying silhouette and massing, presenting an ever-changing, dynamic assemblage of forms, reinforced by color coding.

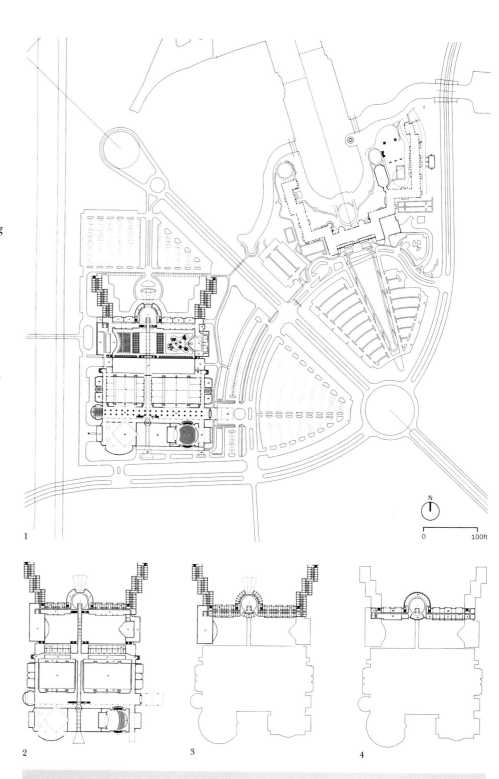

1 Site and ground floor plan
2 Second floor plan
3 Typical floor plan
4 Eighth floor plan
5 Elevation (color rendering)
6 Aerial view of model from park
7 Site model
8 Aerial view of model from access road

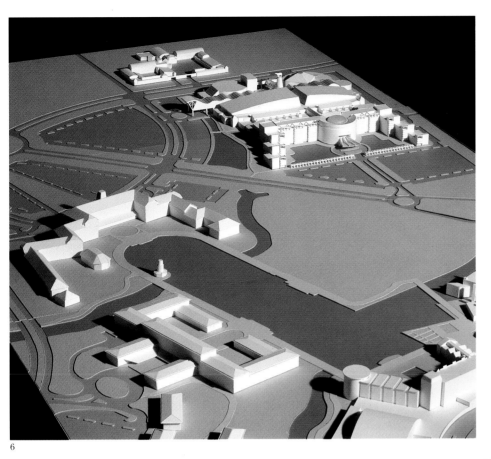

6

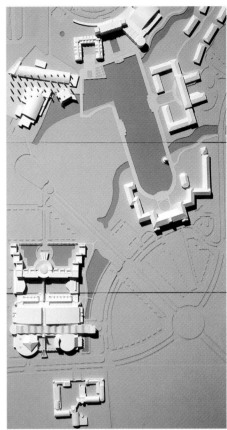

7

8

Henry Art Gallery Renovation and Addition, University of Washington

Design/Completion 1993/1997
Seattle, Washington
University of Washington, Henry Art Gallery
49,000 square feet
Precast concrete panels, board-formed concrete, textured stainless steel, aluminum windows and skylights
Terrazzo, maple panels

The central issue in this project is that of intervention into an existing context and the multiple ramifications that arise. Replication is not an option. The history of architecture has always been enriched through change and dialogue: additions to, interventions in, and renovations of existing buildings. The formal question is: how to reinforce and enrich the original through a comprehensive and interpretive intervention, understanding both the history and the formal implications, as well as being able to analyze the existing conditions, to foster a positive interpretation?

In the case of the Henry Art Gallery, the intent was to maintain and enhance the presence, solidity, and density of the original small masonry building, which was overwhelmed by two large adjacent buildings and compromised by a pedestrian bridge that was perpendicular and tangential to the front facade, diminishing the entry and its sense of place on the site.

From the outset, the fundamental idea was to recast the existing landscaped, bermed site into a new campus entry that added content, context, expectation, and significant visual penetration, reinforcing both the existing statue of George Washington and the facade of the Suzzallo Library, which defined the center of the campus. Also, there was a determined intention to separate the existing Henry Art Gallery and the new addition from the neighboring structures, affording a legitimate transition, an architecturally defined new sense of place, an expectant and enriched entry sequence, an integrated site/circulation/building context that simultaneously engaged art and architecture.

The addition is formed in response to the existing building, the site, and the program. In one sense, the formal idea begins with a linear structure set behind and parallel to the existing building, between it and the existing wall of the underground parking structure. In order to afford pedestrian site penetration, a portion of the linear structure was "compressed" below grade, leaving fragments of the original, in the form

Continued

1

2

3

1   Aerial view
2   Original building and addition from pedestrian bridge
3   View of addition over skylights from plaza
4   Site plan
5   Site section
6   Entrance from Red Square

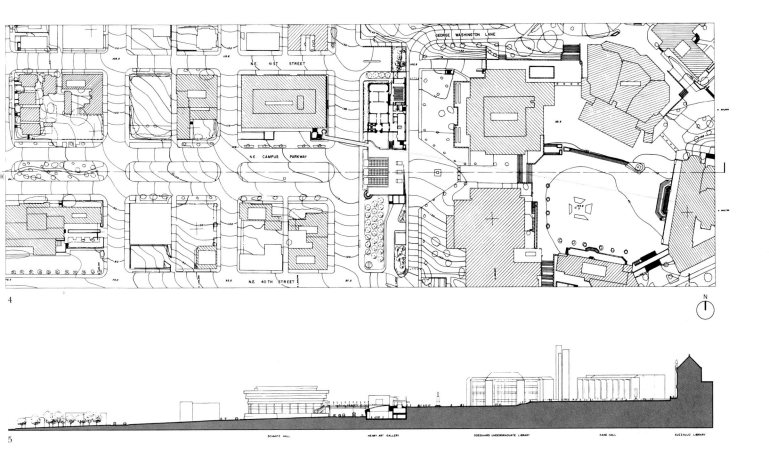

4

5

6

of three skylights which articulate the "gatelike" porosity of the site, as well as affording natural light to the administrative offices below. From this compressed and limited site, the remainder of the building is extruded forward to 15th Avenue in the curved roofed form to accentuate the silhouette, the foothill nature of the site, and the counterpoint to the original Henry, and as a memorable form to be re-experienced from within, as the new main gallery.

In another sense, one could describe the result as a carving away of a solid to reveal composite fragments, all interacting with the original Henry to resite it, as the asymmetrical though primary object, in a new contextual frame that unifies the multiple site and architectural issues at the end of Campus Parkway.

Finally, the result could also be defined as an architectural collage, unifying disparate elements in both counterpointal and asymmetrical variations that ultimately re-establish the primary site axis to Suzzallo Library, reconcile the vertical transition from 15th Avenue to the plaza level, and integrate the original Henry facade with the new sculpture court and entry to the campus and the museum. The forms, as fragments, are implicit in their implications as spaces, but being abstract in their ambiguity to not directly reveal that space. Thus, a sense of anticipation, sequential revelation, and memory becomes as crucial to the experience as the fact.

7

8

9

10

11 Level three plan
12 Level two plan
13 Level one plan
14 Main stair on cross axis to entry of original building
15&16 Main gallery

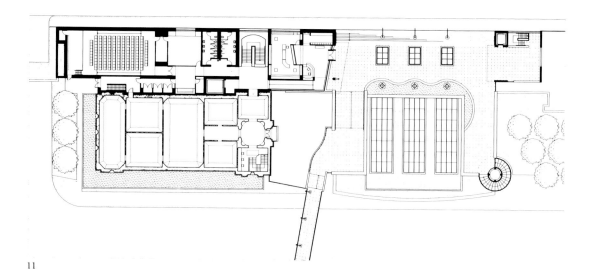

11

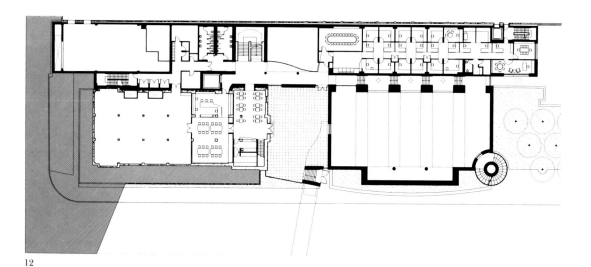

12

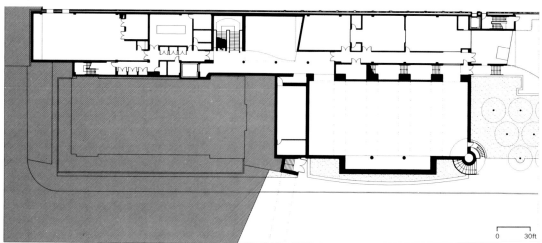

0   30ft

13

14

15

16

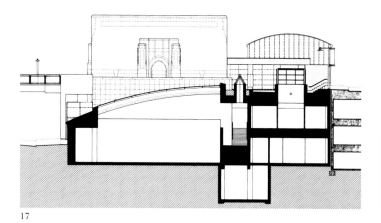

17

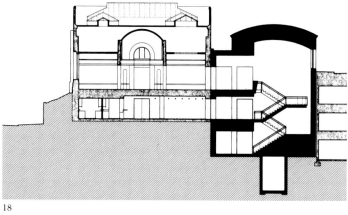

18

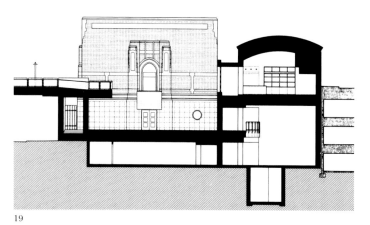

19

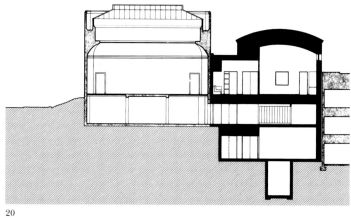

20

21

22

23

24

25

26&27   Northeast double-height gallery
  28   Main gallery
  29   Restored entry rotunda of original building

26

27

28

29

Hilltop Residence

Design/Completion 1992/1997
Austin, Texas
Private owner
28,000 square feet
Granite, stucco, lead-coated copper, stainless steel, steel windows
Integral color plaster walls, maple, cherry, granite, limestone and
greenstone floors, pearwood millwork, pearwood and maple cabinetwork

This residence is located on a wooded hilltop site with views of downtown Austin and the University of Texas. The parti exemplifies the idea of a building in, rather than on, the landscape. By raising the grade on the east side of the site, the transformation of "carving" the building/site as an integrated engagement enriches the total experience, as well as redefining the usual "house on top of the hill."

The program's primary focus is on family life, with secondary emphasis on entertainment and conference functions. The building is organized around a horizontal spine, with the "family house" to the northwest and the "entertainment house" to the southeast. These components are treated as complex figural objects within the landscape.

The building defines the site on the west by horizontal extension at the lower level and upper level entry courts, on the south by a lower level play court, and on the east by expansive lawn and pool terraces. A two-story covered arcade engages the lawn/terrace area and connects the main house on the north to the entertainment/guest house on the south.

The full extent of the house is visible only from the air. From the ground it reads as layers of integrated building and landscape fragments comprehended only through memory and speculation as one moves around the site from inside to outside.

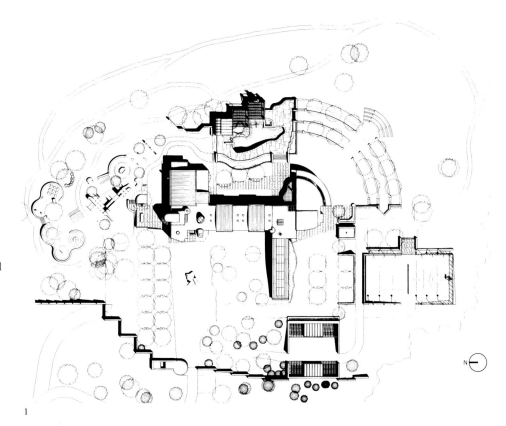

1

2

1 Site plan
2 Aerial view looking south
3 Site model

3

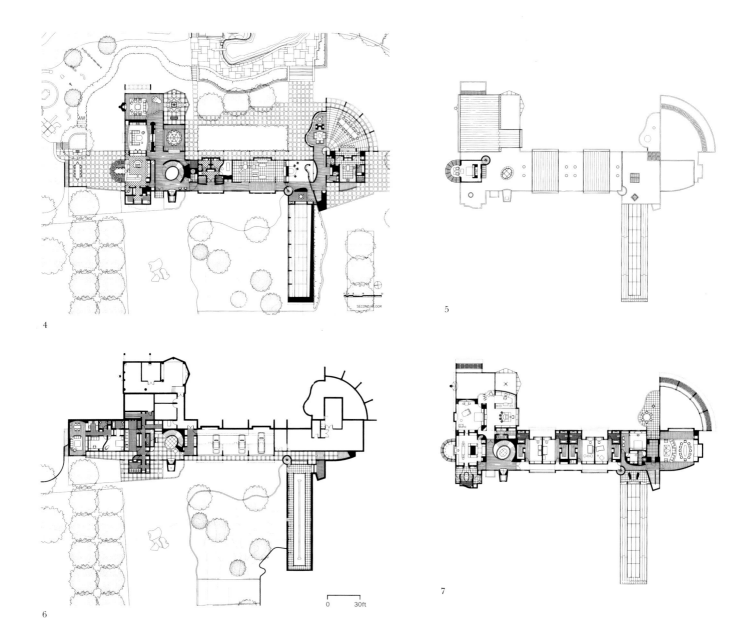

4   0   30ft

4   Second floor plan
5   Fourth floor plan
6   First floor plan
7   Third floor plan
8   Aerial view looking southeast
9   Aerial view looking west

8

9

The Museum of Contemporary Art

Design/Completion 1993/1996
North Miami, Florida
The Museum of Contemporary Art
23,000 square feet
Painted stucco, groundfaced concrete block,
galvanized corrugated metal panels, steel

This modest museum is situated between City Hall and the proposed Police Headquarters, transforming an existing parking lot into an urban art plaza and redefining the town center as a cultural complex.

The building is composed of four articulated and interconnected elements which are assembled as a composition of cubist objects to form a dynamic visual collage that provokes curiosity, engagement, and an appreciation of both art and architecture.

The structure frames an exterior sculpture courtyard which provides pedestrian circulation to all parts of the museum, and creates a visual dialogue between the Police Building and City Hall. The public plaza is outlined by a 28-foot grid of 40-foot-high palm trees at 125th Street, and by the reflecting pool, studio, and museum entry arcade on the south side.

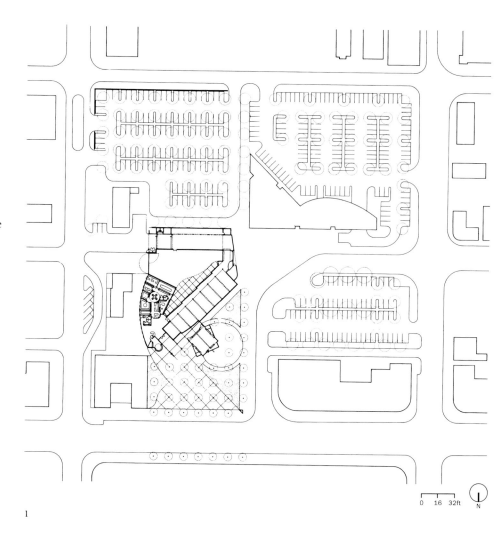

1

0 16 32ft

2

1 Site plan
2 Entry facade across public plaza
3 West entry arcade detail
4 Detail of west gallery corner with studio in background
5 Axonometric
6 East facade with museum store and entry arcade

3

4

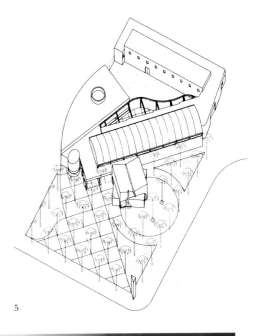

5

6

7

8

9

10

Nanyang Polytechnic

Completion 1992 (phase 1) 1999 (phase 2)
Ang Mo Kio (North-Central region), Singapore
Singapore Government Ministry of Education
2,300,000 square feet
Reinforced concrete, steel, painted stucco, ceramic tile,
aluminum window system

Nanyang Polytechnic is located on a
75-acre site in North Central Singapore.
Serving 12,000 students, it is a 2.3-million-
square-foot interactive educational
community which extends to the north
and south from a central multi-use core
of common facilities, inspired by the
"town square" model.

A system of cloisters and covered walkways
provide access to the four schools and to
all administrative and common-use
facilities. The circulation system integrates
the covered outdoor terraces and is
designed to form a series of landscaped
outdoor spaces, gardens, and courtyards
which offer a multiplicity of visual
references and provide a sense of
orientation.

The major pedestrian entranceway from
the public transportation hub is designed
as an extension of the covered walkway
principle, providing direct access to the
central multi-use core and gateways to
each school, including easy access for the
handicapped. It is also vertically separated
from the campus road system.

The daily process of arrival, circulation,
and return is a designed sequence and
procession of varied visual and functional
experiences. The overall organization
integrates architecture, outdoor space,
and pedestrian circulation systems that are
psychologically uplifting and inspirational.

Circulation is conceived as a circular loop
system without dead ends. Multiple
options are available, but the primary
route from the main entrance to all
functions is direct and logical.

The vehicular circulation system is
designed to be independent of the
pedestrian system; all crossings are grade-
separated. The primary entrance for
visiting VIPs is the Grand Entrance Plaza
and covered drop-off, which is overlaid
above the public transportation pedestrian
entrance and the landscaped water
courtyard.

Continued

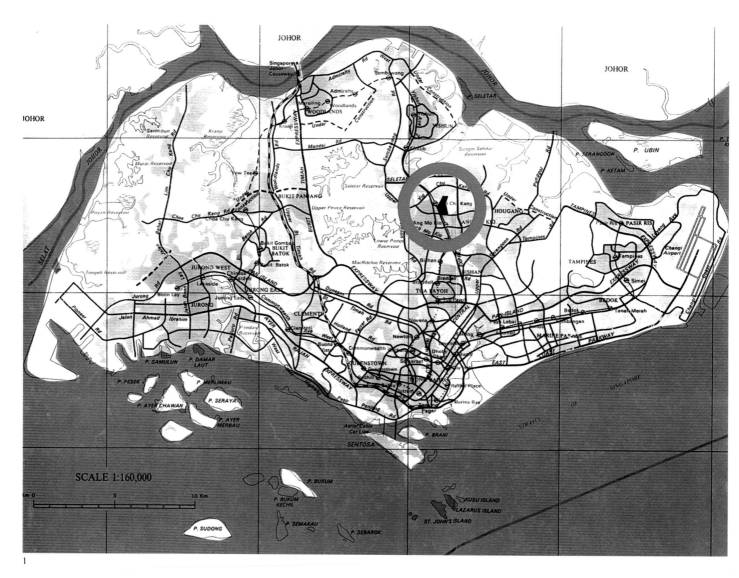

1

1   Map of Singapore showing site (circled)
2   Pedestrian circulation
3   Campus Center
4   Sports, facility, and student center
5   Vehicular circulation
6   Facility housing
7   Future expansion sites

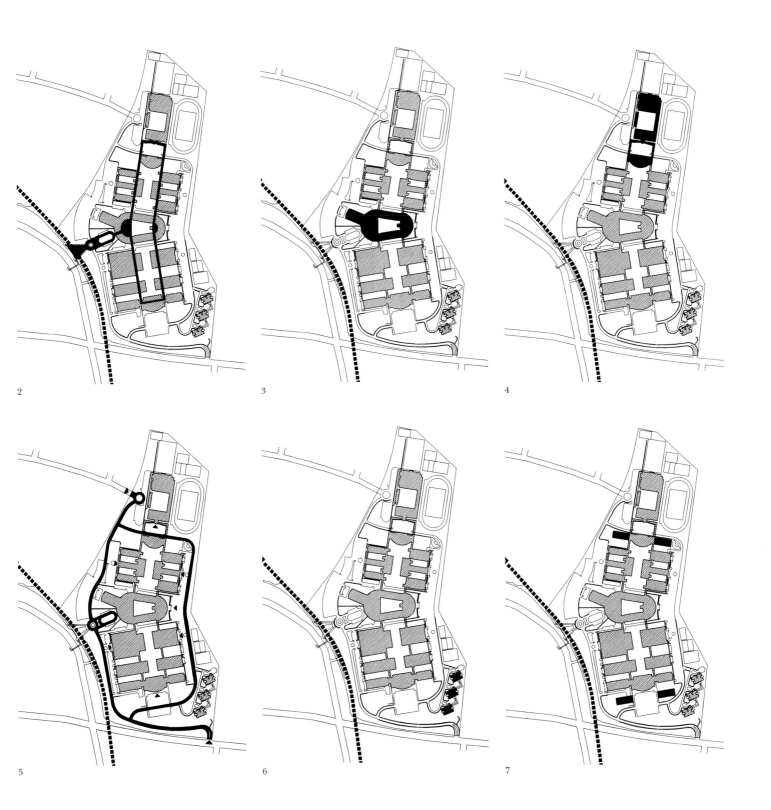

2

3

4

5

6

7

Parking and visitor drop-off points are provided at each school and common-use facility. Parking lots are distributed along the perimeter loop road and are landscaped with groves of trees which provide shade as well as defining the east–west boundaries of the campus. Services are provided at the lowest level of the Campus Center and are accessed by a dedicated loop road system.

The three campus levels are sympathetic to the existing topography thereby minimizing earthworks. The low-level western side provides vehicle access to the School of Engineering, the School of Business Management, the main central core, and the sports facilities. The middle level, which includes the Student Activity Center and gardens, provides access to lecture theaters, canteens, child care, and the staff center. The upper-level eastern side provides access to the School of Information Technology, the School of Health Science, and level 3 of the Campus Center.

The middle-level gardens contain common-use spaces and form a north–south "green spine." The specific schools are located to the east and west of the spine and terminate at the perimeter parking lots. All main facades and window areas are oriented to the north and south to minimize solar heat gain and are provided with external sun control overhangs. Athletic fields are oriented north–south and grandstands to the east.

The Campus Center building is organized around a central terraced garden which is designed to allow for air movement, natural ventilation and daylight, making the space comfortable for a wide range of functions. Covered perimeter cloisters provide sheltered circulation during inclement weather. The multi-use building is cost-effective, combining functions which are often designed as separate buildings.

Continued

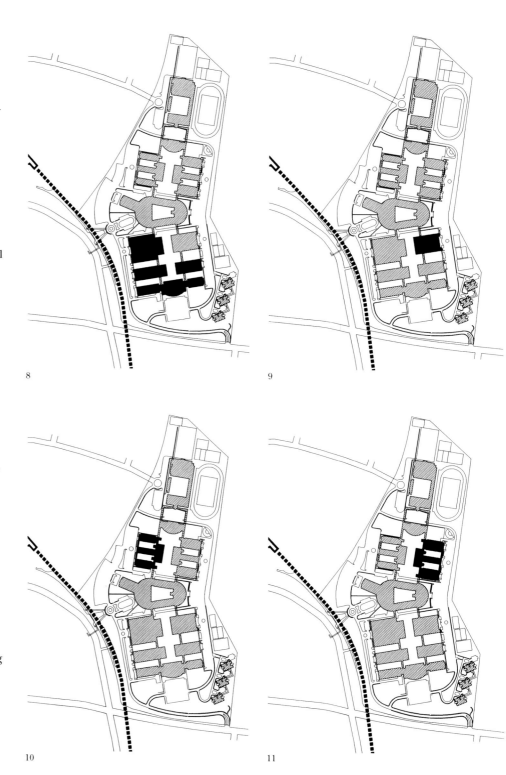

8

9

10

11

180

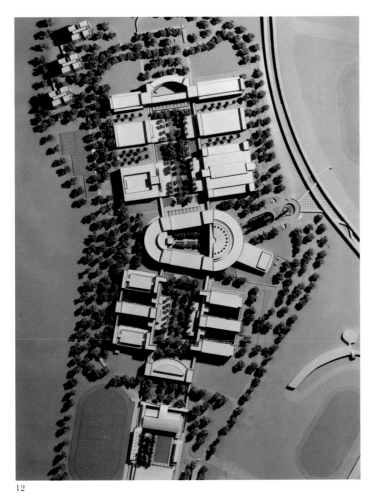

12

13

14

The library is located on levels 4 and 5 of the Campus Center building, convenient to the main entrance, central to all schools, and oriented to the gardens to its north, south, and center. The auditorium is located at the primary vehicle plaza and public transportation connection, making it accessible to both public and school functions. Staff housing is located at the eastern edge, separated from the center campus, with dedicated parking areas.

The buildings which house the required program for specific-use spaces are efficient and easy to construct and have logical structures. On the exterior facades, a combination of painted stucco and large-scale ceramic tile finish is used as a low-maintenance lower wall as well as a decorative device to integrate color and texture.

The gardens and courtyards are proposed as decorative outdoor spaces defined by the surrounding building facades. The multiplicity and variety of these spaces allow the campus to have a complexity and architectural presence which is visually stimulating yet cost-effective.

The pedestrian and vehicular circulation networks provide expansion sites to allow for 25 percent growth. Each school has its own provision for expansion, which can proceed on independent schedules.

The mission of Nanyang Polytechnic is to bring together business, industry, and education. Its purpose is also to promote intellectual development and reinforce the essential work ethic. The unique appearance and flexible functional characteristics of the Campus Center, the synergistic organization of the campus plan, and the specific program of workshop, specialist center, and industrial project center spaces devised for this polytechnic provide an environment and image capable of achieving this mission. Meaningful architectural complexes have invariably established a "sense of place and memory." The varied and composite program of Nanyang Polytechnic affords an architecture of presence, aspiration, and identity.

15

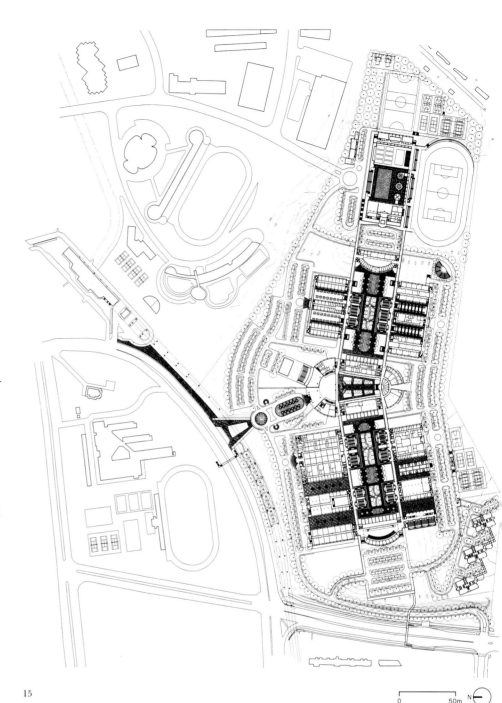

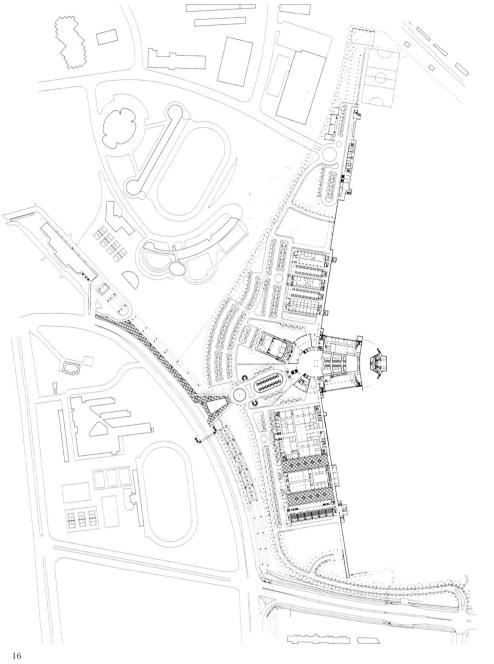

15   Main level plan
16   Entry level plan
17   Composite plan of Campus Center

16

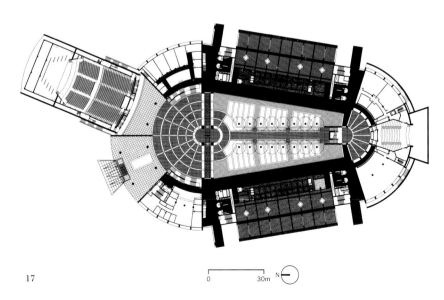

17

0   30m   N

18

19

20

21

22

23

24

25

26

21 International Holdings Inc. Offices

Design/Completion 1993/1994
New York, New York
21 International Holdings Inc.
14,000 square feet
Maple ceilings, wall paneling, doors, ducks, and floors; beige marble floors; cherry cabinetwork; plaster walls; brushed aluminum ceilings

21 International Holdings is a multifaceted investment company whose 14,000-square-foot corporate offices in the Seagram Building house a 3,000-square-foot chairman's suite, executive offices, foundation offices, and support spaces. The central design constraints were the building's landmark status and lease-mandated restrictions on interior renovations. The elevator lobby envelope was unalterable, as were the luminous ceiling with its 4-foot square grid and the perimeter walls, which required a minimum of 5 feet between them and the built-in furniture.

The design perceptually renders the space as "carved away" to reveal its archaeological precedents. The offices are read as a construction within a construction; the architects' interventions work in a point–counterpoint dialogue with the original elements of Mies's design. The luminous ceiling is treated as a constant plane of reference; interior walls are capped with a 12-inch-high glass transom that defines the limits of the new design and marks the transition from intervention to original construction.

The circulation space establishes the referential and dynamic aesthetic. The vertical/sectional articulation reinforces the hierarchical uses: reception, circulation, workstations, and perimeter office entries.

The subtle palette of colors and materials provides a strategic environment for unique pieces of furniture and objects of art. These include a dozen Hoffmann chairs, an Art Deco desk, Secessionist silver selected by the architect and client specifically for the space, and pieces from Chairman Marshall Cogan's private collection.

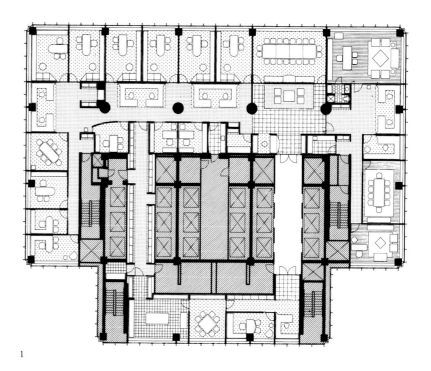

1

2

186

3

4 Secretarial station outside chairman's office
5 Reception area
6 Principals' dining room
7 Boardroom with custom-designed table
8 Chairman's office

4

5

6

7

8

San Onofre Residence

Design/Completion 1993/1997
Pacific Palisades, California
Private owner
15,000 square feet
Cleft-cut limestone, stucco, zinc metal panels, standing seam zinc roof,
elastometric PVC membranes, insulated laminated glass

This private residence is located on 1.5 acres at the end of Malibu Canyon. The two-level site suggested a binuclear parti. A three-story curved limestone pavilion, housing the main living spaces, sits on a promontory looking south and east towards Santa Monica, the Pacific Ocean, and the skyline of downtown Los Angeles. A three-story cube containing support space is embedded in the slope behind, overlooking the canyon to the west.

The canyon building is designed as an object in the landscape, anchoring and stabilizing the pavilion yet separate and unique in its organization and rendering. The curved limestone is intended to read as both a found object and a ruin, transforming the ordered disposition of the support building into an explosion of space and vistas revealed by the pavilion's glazed facade.

One enters on both levels between two elements in a horizontal and vertical circulation space facing the canyon to the west. The pavilion houses a double-height living room with views to Santa Monica and the Pacific Ocean. The kitchen and the master bedroom unite as an object that floats within the space of the pavilion, separating the living room from the dining room. The breakfast room penetrates the screen of the glazed facade and creates an outdoor terrace for the bedroom above. At ground level, the entertainment room becomes a giant *piloti*; recessed in the curve of the pavilion, it provides a shaded area near the swimming pool.

The canyon building is organized bilaterally and accommodates the exercise room on the ground level, the guest bedrooms at entry level, and an office/conference suite above at the master bedroom level. In the core, a screening room and archival library occupy the ground level. On the third level, the master dressing room and bathroom, opposite the offices, are rotated on axis with the bridge that returns to the pavilion.

The juxtaposition of shapes and textures creates a Cubist bas-relief, reiterated by an unexpected use of traditional and modern materials.

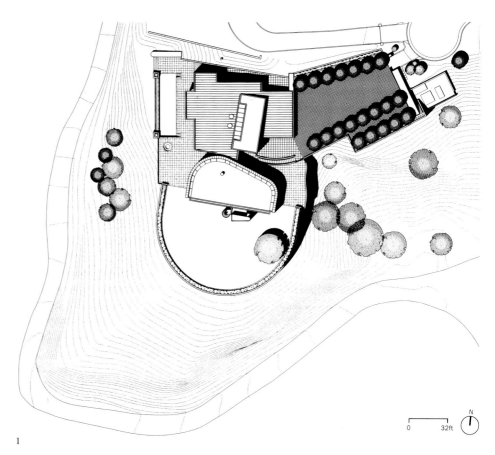

1

2

1 Site plan
2 View of south facade
Opposite:
    Detail of east terrace entrance

190

4

5

4   Front entry
5   Northwest view of pool terrace
6–9 Axonometric views
10 View of southeast corner looking north
11 Southwest pool terrace towards mountains

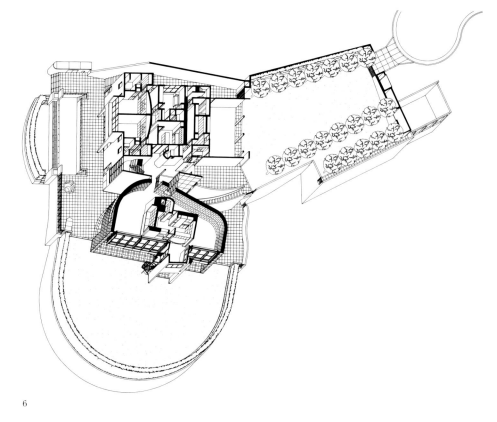

6

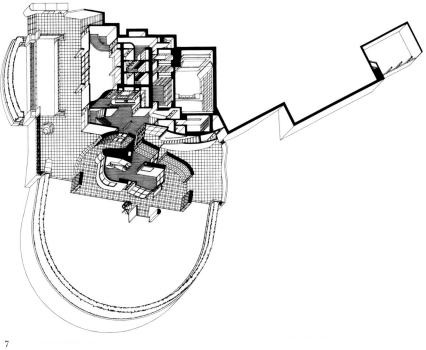

7

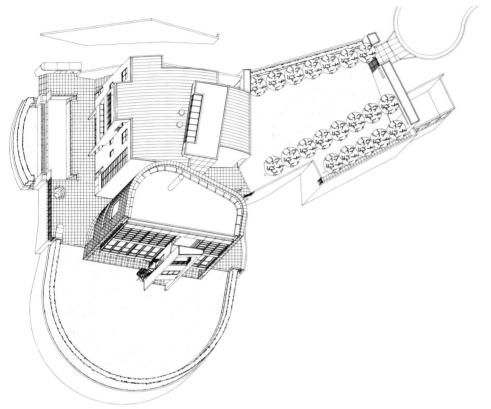

8

10

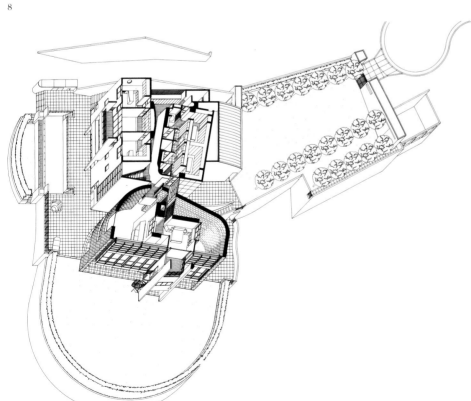

9

11

12

13

14

15

16

17

18

15   Living room
16   Dining room
17   Main stair from third floor: view towards mountains
18   Master bedroom
Opposite:
    Northwest view of pool terrace at dusk

Institute for Human Performance, Rehabilitation and Biomedical Research, State University of New York at Syracuse

Design/Completion 1990/1999
Syracuse, New York
State University Construction Fund
200,000 square feet
Steel and concrete deck, brick, cast stone, aluminum panels, curtain wall
Plaster, tiles, special athletics surfaces

This facility for education, research, and patient care is a four-story structure accommodating a 19,000-square-foot gymnasium and track, a 75-foot-long medical research and rehabilitation swimming pool with a hydraulic floor, a full-service orthopedic treatment center, and 100 state-of-the-art flexible laboratory modules.

The building is divided into three parallel laboratory wings joined by two skylit atriums. The wings house research units grouped into laboratory modules and designed for maximum efficiency and flexibility in mechanical and utility configurations.

The two atriums bring controlled natural light into the main entrance and circulation space at ground level, the public gymnasium at the second level, and the laboratories at the third and fourth levels. They also establish the major public volumes by articulating the entrance and the gymnasium. Views from the laboratory windows across to the opposite wings and below to public spaces enhance a sense of community and create a collegiate atmosphere.

The design, which evolved from precise and extensive technical criteria, provides climate-controlled spaces for multiple medical and recreational functions. Public and private domains are expressed by manipulation of the light and the solid–void relationships.

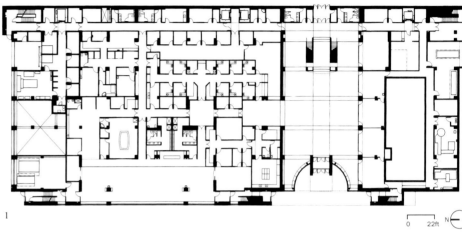

1

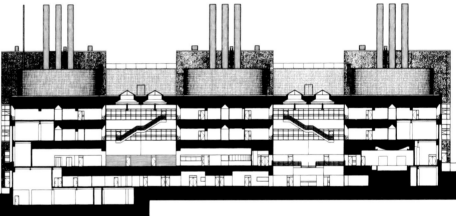

2

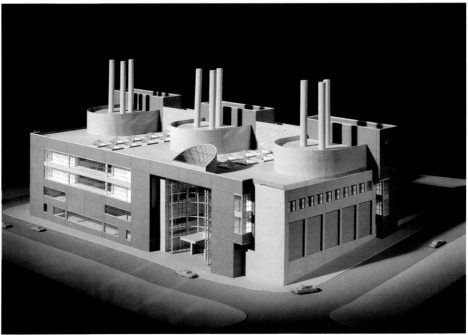

3

4

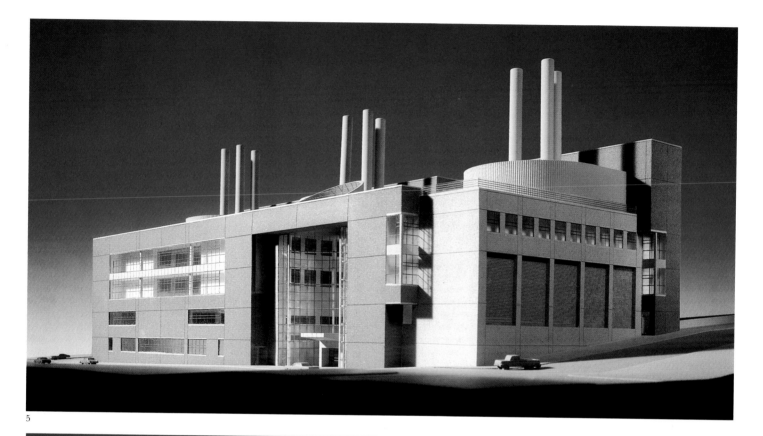

5

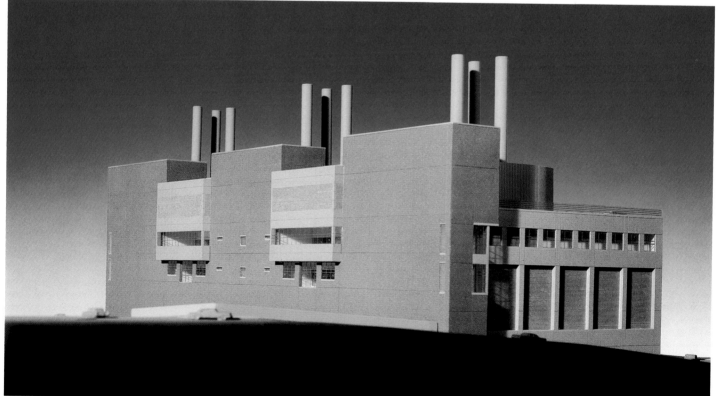

6

Levitt Center for University Advancement, University of Iowa

Design/Completion 1993/1997
Iowa City, Iowa
University of Iowa Foundation
120,000 square feet
Indiana limestone, white aluminum panels, glass block, aluminum bris soliel, exposed concrete
Terrazzo floors, maple, cherry millwork

Located on a steep hill at the northern edge of the University of Iowa's Fine Arts campus, opposite City Park and overlooking the Iowa River to the south and west, the Levitt Center for University Advancement acts as both a visual and literal gateway to the university.

The new facility accommodates the University of Iowa Foundation and the Alumni Association. It provides offices, meeting spaces, reception, and entertainment facilities for activities that advance the university's goals of fundraising, economic development, publicity, media relations, and alumni services.

The center's visibility and easy accessibility from the main auto approach make it an ideal location for an informal "welcome center," orienting visitors to the campus.

The building is a composite and asymmetrical assemblage of geometric forms that articulate a specific site strategy as well as a programmatic hierarchy. Visible from many parts of the city, particularly when lit at night, the glass-block rotunda and sloped-roof assembly halls anchor the limestone and metal office element, creating a silhouette and a presence on the landscape.

The rotunda provides the main lobby and exhibition gallery, a three-story reception space, and a two-story boardroom suite. The Grand Promenade on level 4 acts as the spine of the office "bar," connecting the boardroom suite with three large assembly halls and staff dining areas. The assembly halls are the building's primary facilities for large-scale meetings, receptions, and dinners. Their curved ceilings create dramatic interior spaces which are lit by high east-facing windows and floor-to-ceiling south-facing window walls opening to the roof terrace.

Levels 1, 2, and 3 of the linear "bar" element are occupied by offices, conference rooms, research and records centers, a library, and other administrative functions. Support services are located in the base of the building.

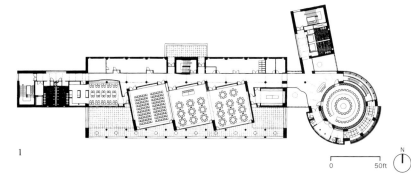

1

0   50ft   N

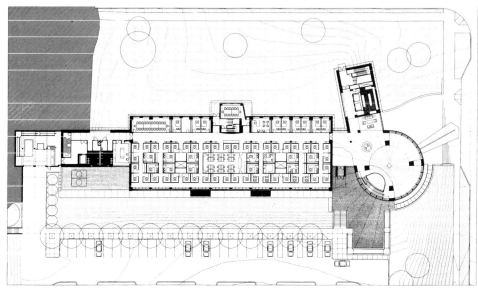

2

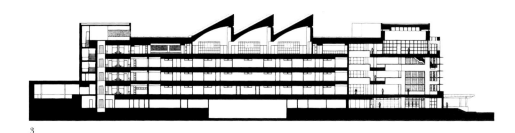

3

4

5

Five plazas and terraces provide for outdoor entertaining and special events. The Entry Plaza allows access to the main reception and exhibit gallery. One level above, the South Rotunda Court leads from the visitor parking to the main level of the rotunda. On the southern side of level 4, a terrace the length of the linear element commands views of the Arts campus along the west bank of the Iowa River, as well as much of the east campus. The north roof terrace overlooks the park, while the boardroom terrace is oriented towards the Iowa River and the old Capitol dome.

6

7

PaceWildenstein Gallery

Design/Completion 1994/1995
Beverly Hills, California
PaceWildenstein
10,000 square feet
Black granite, stainless steel, ardex concrete and carpet floors,
Formica cabinetwork, painted plaster walls

This new gallery is housed in three separate buildings at the intersection of Wilshire Boulevard and Rodeo Drive.

The entrance opening, situated in the first building on a narrow pedestrian alley off Rodeo Drive, was enlarged to reveal a street presence.

The reception area mediates a change in level between the entrance and the ground floor exhibition space in the second building. The walls of the 17-foot-high volume are rotated from the column grid to maximize uninterrupted wall surfaces. A wide stair leads to a mezzanine overlooking the main floor, lit by six new windows punched into the facade.

A stair from the mezzanine leads to another gallery on the second floor of the third building. A grid of existing columns and beams is used to modulate the long space into a series of more intimate rooms suitable for exhibiting smaller work, such as drawings and photography.

Along the perimeter of the building, a floating wall is brought forward by a single row of glass blocks at either end, and stops at the underside of the beams. Lit from behind, the wall controls natural light from the five existing windows and creates an interior hanging surface and a street facade for the gallery.

Behind and beyond the exhibition area are private offices and viewing rooms, accessible from the viewing gallery and from a separate elevator lobby.

1 Second level private reception and waiting area
2 Front entrance to gallery off Rodeo Drive
3 Front reception desk
4 View of ground floor gallery from mezzanine
5 Ground floor sculpture and painting gallery

1

3

2

4

5

6   Second level plan
7   Ground level plan
8   Director's office
9   Entrance to picture gallery from private reception area
10 Private reception desk and waiting area
11 Second floor drawing and picture gallery

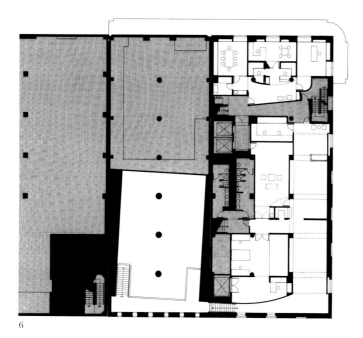

6

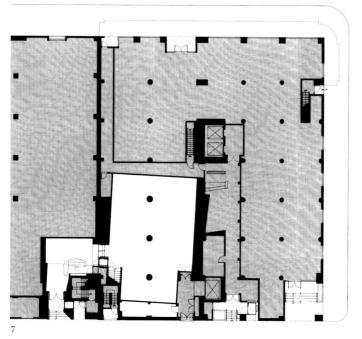

7

8

9

10

11

Physics Building, Princeton University

Design/Completion 1995/1997
Princeton, New Jersey
43,000 square feet (construction); 10,000 square feet (renovation)
Brick, cast stone, stucco, zinc shingles, zinc standing seam walls and roof, aluminum windows, glass, glass block, exposed concrete

This undergraduate teaching center connects the existing Physics and Mathematics buildings. One of the first campus buildings visible from the main auto approach, the new center engages the existing buildings, creating a "gateway" to the campus. Framed by Fine Tower to the north and Jadwin Hall to the south, the building also acts as a visual terminus to College Walk, the east–west pedestrian axis.

Three major programmatic divisions—lecture halls, classrooms, and labs—are articulated through their massing and materials as three separate elements. Two lecture halls are located primarily below ground, forming a "base" for two "objects:" a cast stone element that faces the plaza, containing five classrooms and service areas; and a zinc-clad element rotated to the axis of College Walk, containing six technology laboratories and adjacent classrooms. The public circulation acts as a "wrapper" connecting the "objects."

At level 1, a canopy marks the entrance to a double-height atrium with access to five classrooms and three laboratories. The atrium connects the new building with Jadwin Hall. On level 2, the barrel-vaulted ceilings of three additional laboratories allow experiments involving height. An exterior stair leads down to a second entrance on level A, where an existing gallery was refurbished to create lobby space for two new lecture halls. The steeply raked halls are provided with rear projection facilities, catwalks, and turntable stages, which allow large-scale experiments to be set up in the prep space behind the stage and then rotated into the lecture halls. All three buildings are linked at level A, allowing multiple access to the lecture halls.

The exterior "base" is clad in alternating bands of black and gray wire-cut brick to complement adjacent buildings and to articulate the floor, ceiling, and window

Continued

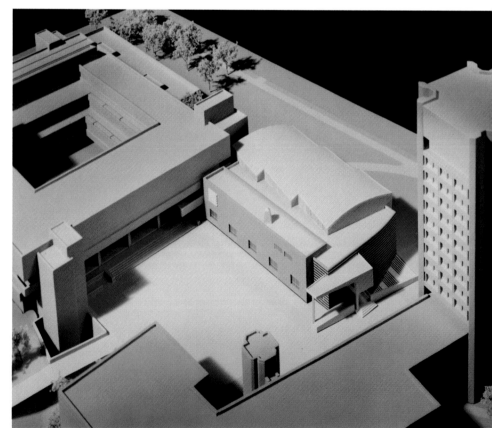

1

2

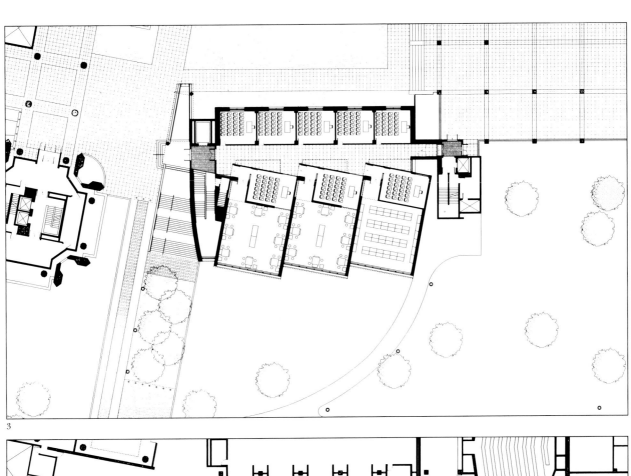

3

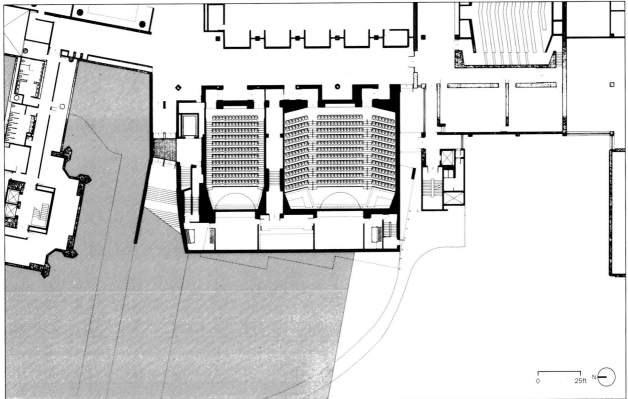

4

0   25ft   N

data of the new building. The barrel-vaulted roof of the lab element, which is visible from adjacent buildings, is treated as a fifth facade and is clad in standing seam zinc. The walls of the lab are also clad in standing seam zinc panels and zinc shingles, further articulating it as the "object" in the existing contextual frame. The plaza element is faced with cast stone to continue the granite and masonry courtyard enclosure of the existing buildings.

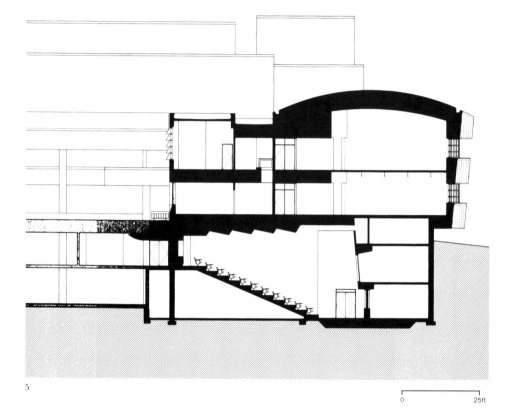

5

0   25ft

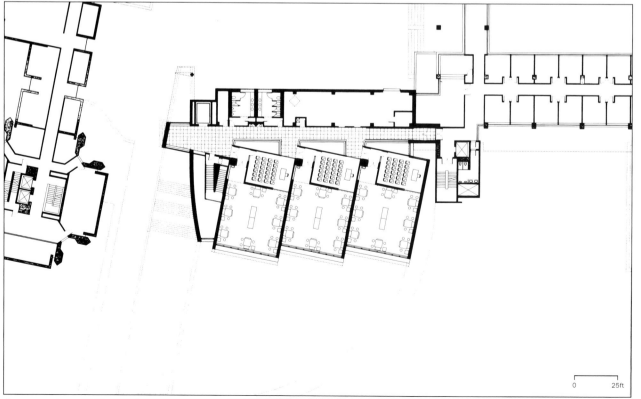

0   25ft

6

7

8

9

10

5   Section
6   Level 2 context
7   Roof level viewed from Fine Tower
8   View from northeast
9   View from northwest
10 View from southwest looking towards Fine Tower

Meyer Residence

Design/Completion 1995/1999
Malibu, California
Private owner
14,700 square feet
Stucco, zinc roof and copings, stainless steel railings, thermal finish
limestone pavers, bluestone cobble driveway, teak windows and doors
Mahogany doors and cabinets, ebonized incensio wood floors, teak decks

This private residence is located on a 3-acre site defined by the Pacific Coast Highway to the north and the Pacific Ocean to the south. Two-story residences define the east and west boundaries. The program requirements included a main house and garage, a swimming pool and pool house, a guest house, and a tennis court. Interlocking building volumes and outdoor spaces are layered within the framework of the site, resulting in an ordered sequence of transitional spaces.

London plane trees line the entry drive defining the western boundary of the site, while a landscaped grove of pear trees provides shelter for the guest parking and screens the guest house and tennis court to the east. The drive terminates in an autocourt which acts as a transition between the guest house/lawn area and the north side of the main house. The main house, swimming pool, and pool house are located at the southern edge of the site, parallel to the bluff and the ocean. To maximize views, the living/dining/kitchen area and master bedroom are elevated to the second floor and are organized under a gull wing roof, which provides a continuous inverted vault ceiling for these spaces.

Continued

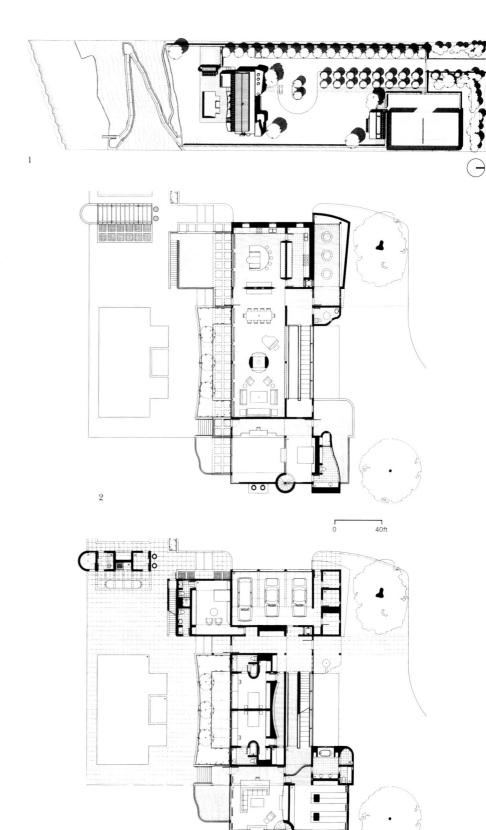

1

N

0   40ft

2

1 Site plan
2 Second level plan
3 First level plan
4 View of driveway entrance looking south

3

At ground level, the entry separates the garage and service areas from the children's bedrooms, and allows direct access to the pool terrace and the nanny's bedroom. A circulation stair/ramp runs parallel to the two-story exterior glazed wall, connecting both full and half levels of the house. The lower level contains the screening room, exercise room, and service and mechanical areas. The ramp leads from the entry to the first half level and is terminated by the master bedroom. A spiral stair leads to a sleeping loft oriented towards the ocean, and overlooking the double-height sitting room below. The second floor provides a loft-like sequence of kitchen/dining/living spaces, with open southern views of the coastline and ocean, as well as a playroom/studio on the north side with views over the site.

The parti combines an open pavilion and private spaces within a prescribed area and height limit by inventive manipulations of section and circulation.

5

5 View of driveway and entry court looking southwest
6 View of pool terrace looking northwest
7 View of pool terrace looking northeast

6

University Technology and Learning Complex, Lawrence Technological University

Design/Completion 1997/1999
Southfield, Michigan
120,000 square feet
Painted aluminum panels, clear and frosted insulating glass, stucco, painted steel standing seam roofs

The new building is an educational facility for the study of architecture, engineering, interior design, and object design. The program includes state-of-the-art electronic, computer, and learning facilities; expanded studios and laboratories; galleries and lecture rooms; an office of the future; a resource center with a 15,000-volume library; and classrooms, conference rooms, and office spaces. The complex will renovate and expand the current Architecture Building and provide an enclosed link to the existing Engineering Building.

Vehicular traffic will be redirected around the campus perimeter; landscape design will redefine the main quadrangle, adding a dramatic new gateway to the campus from the Ten Mile Road entrance.

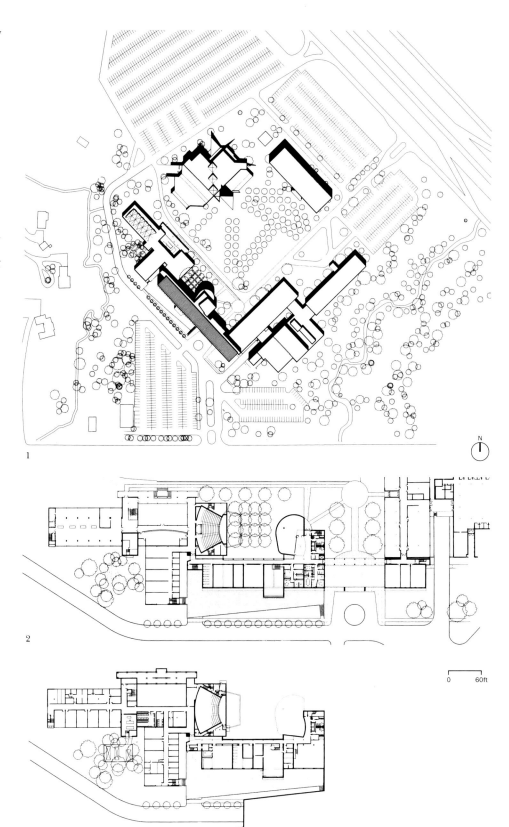

1   Site plan
2   Second floor plan
3   First floor plan
4   North elevation
5   South elevation
6   South elevation looking west
7   Section
8   North elevation looking west
9   North elevation looking east

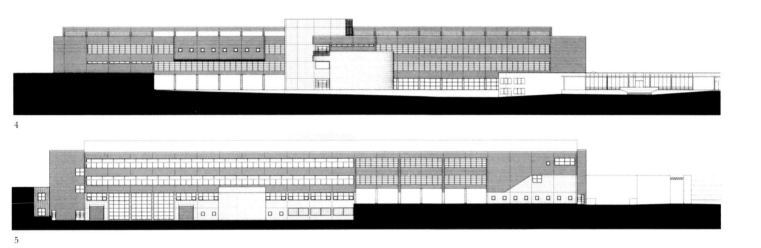

4

5

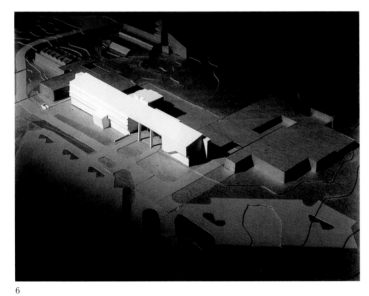

6

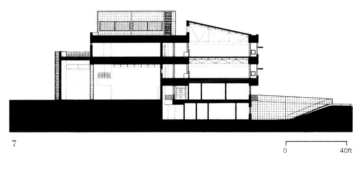

7

8

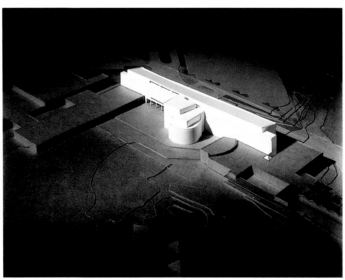

9

Baker Library, Graduate School of Business Administration, Harvard University

Design/Completion 1996/2001
Cambridge, Massachusetts
Harvard University
160,000 square feet
Brick, stone, steel

Baker Library was designed by McKim, Mead & White Architects in 1925 and is situated in the heart of the Harvard Business School campus. The renovation and addition address the complex integration of the traditional study library, the modern electronic library, and a dynamic new vision of a globally linked teaching and meeting facility. The design will create a strong new visual image that remains contextually sensitive to the site while offering a new main south entry quad.

The renovation includes the main Reading Room, the Aldrich Reading Room and the Rare Books Library. New facilities include four multi-use gathering spaces, book stacks, a computer commons and cafe, conference/meeting rooms, library staff offices, and a multimedia television studio.

The dominant image of the new south facade is the rotunda, the building's primary entry, meeting, and circulation space. This five-story-high volume is defined by concentric stairs and balconies at each level. The rotunda and the three other gathering spaces—the existing double-height north lobby and two two-story balconied volumes—afford maximum flexibility.

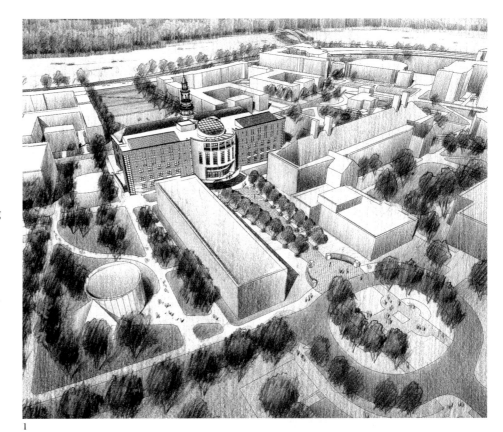

1

1　Aerial view of new south entry quadrangle
2　View from new south entry quadrangle
3　View inside rotunda looking towards new south entry quadrangle
4　View inside rotunda looking north
5　View into rotunda from balcony
6　View into multi-use gathering space from meeting room gallery
7　View into multimedia television studio
8　Sectional view of multimedia television studio

2

3

4

5

6

7

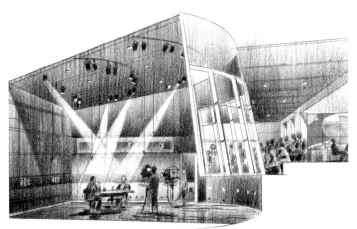

8

Casa Vecchia

Design/Completion 1996/1999
Bel Air, California
Private owner
15,000 square feet
Stucco, stainless steel, steel-framed windows and doors, slate paving

The buildable site, a 2-acre plateau located 60 feet below the access road, affords panoramic views of Westwood, the Pacific Ocean, and the canyon. The program and topography favored a composite courtyard/linear wall parti.

The "head," oriented to the south and west, accommodates the entry, sitting room, living room, and main stair on the ground level, two private studios on the second level, and the master bedroom suite on the third level.

The south wing, perpendicular to the main stair volume, accommodates the dining room and kitchen/breakfast room on the ground floor and the family room and daughter's bedroom on the second floor.

The east wing, perpendicular to the gallery stair, accommodates the garage and service spaces on the ground floor and four bedroom suites on the second floor.

The pool and terrace are located on the eastern portion of the site, extending the outdoor private spaces from the western edge of the site.

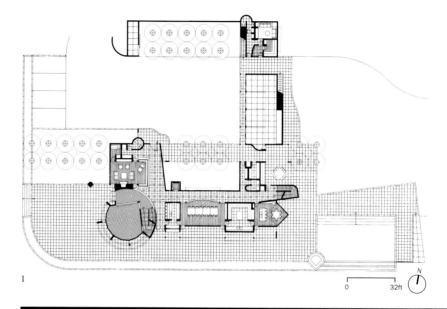

1

2

3

1 First floor plan
2 Southwest elevation
3 Southwest view of living room rotunda
4 Third floor plan
5 Second floor plan
6 Basement plan
7 Northwest view from entry drive
8 Aerial view from southwest
9 Aerial view from southeast

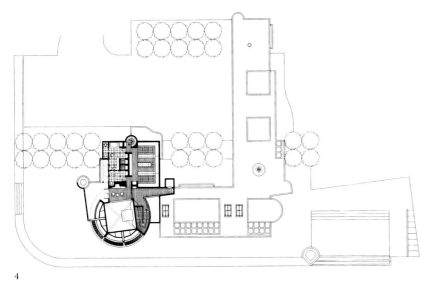

4

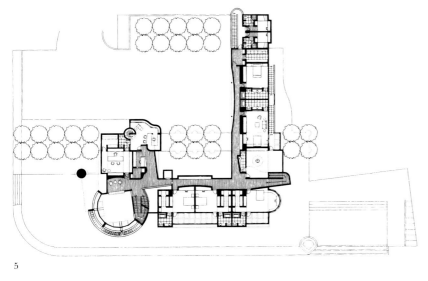

5

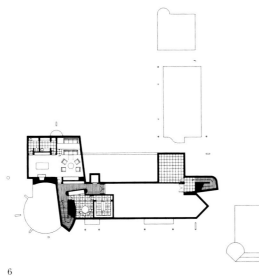

6

7

8

9

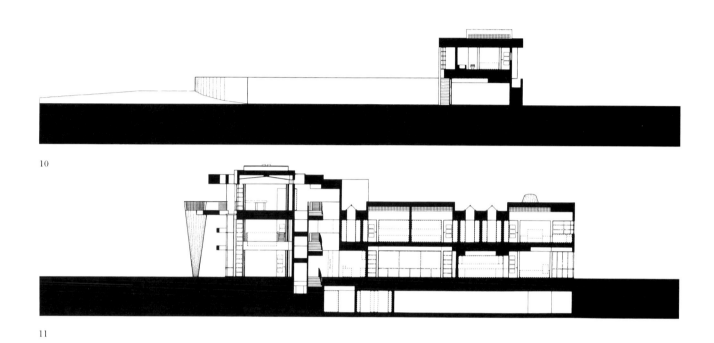

10

11

12

13

14

10   Section through garage and guest bathroom looking north
11   Section through living room and bedrooms looking north
12   Section through bedrooms and gym looking east
13   Section through dining room and bedroom looking east
14   Section through living room looking east
15   South elevation
16   East elevation
17   West elevation

15

16

17

FIRM PROFILE

Gwathmey Siegel & Associates Architects was established in 1967 by Charles Gwathmey and Robert Siegel. Since its foundation the firm has completed over 300 projects, ranging from distinguished cultural and educational facilities, corporate buildings, and office interiors to private houses, furniture and product design.

Gwathmey Siegel & Associates has received 90 awards for design excellence, including the Firm Award—the highest honor of the American Institute of Architects (AIA); the Gold Medal from the AIA New York City Chapter; and the Lifetime Achievement Award from the State of New York.

The work of Gwathmey Siegel & Associates has been published internationally and is recognized and acclaimed world-wide.

Biographies

Charles Gwathmey

Charles Gwathmey attended the University of Pennsylvania School of Architecture from 1956 to 1959. He received his Master of Architecture degree from Yale University in 1962 and was awarded the William Wirt Winchester Fellowship as the outstanding graduate, as well as a Fulbright Grant. During the last 24 years he has held faculty positions at Pratt Institute, Cooper Union, Princeton University, Columbia University, University of Texas, and the University of California at Los Angeles. Gwathmey was Davenport Professor at Yale University in 1983, Eliot Noyes Visiting Professor at Harvard University in 1985, and the Bishop Professor at Yale in 1991.

In 1970 Gwathmey received the Brunner Prize from the American Academy of Arts and Letters, and was elected to membership in 1976. He was President of the Board of Trustees for the Institute of Architecture and Urban Studies and was elected a Fellow of the American Institute of Architects in 1981.

Gwathmey received the Medal of Honor from the New York Chapter of the American Institute of Architects in 1983, and in 1985 he was the first recipient of the Yale Alumni Arts Award from the School of Architecture. In 1988 Gwathmey received the Lifetime Achievement Medal in the Visual Arts from the Guild Hall Academy of the Arts and in 1990 he received the Lifetime Achievement Award from the New York State Society of Architects. In 1994 Gwathmey became a Trustee of the Cooper Union for the Advancement of Science and Art.

Robert Siegel

Robert Siegel received his Bachelor of Architecture degree from Pratt Institute in 1962 and his Master of Architecture degree from Harvard University in 1963.

Siegel was awarded the Medal of Honor from the New York Chapter of the American Institute of Architects in 1983 and the Pratt Institute Centennial Alumni Award in Architecture in 1988. Siegel received the Lifetime Achievement Award from the New York State Society of Architects in 1990, and in 1991 he was elected a Fellow of the American Institute of Architects. Throughout his career, Siegel has served as a design critic, juror, and lecturer at schools of architecture in America and the Far East. He is a Trustee of Pratt Institute.

In 1982 Gwathmey Siegel & Associates Architects received the Firm Award from the American Institute of Architects for "approaching every project with a fresh eye, unswerving dedication to design excellence, and a strong belief in collaborative effort."

Chronological List of Buildings, Projects, Furniture & Objects

* Indicates work featured in this book
(*see Selected and Current Works*).

Charles Gwathmey, Architect

1964

Miller Residence
Fire Island, New York

1965

Herlinger-Bistol Ltd Showrooms and Offices
New York, New York

Gwathmey Residence and Studio
Amagansett, New York

Gwathmey & Henderson Architects

1966

Straus Residence
East Hampton, New York

1967

Sedacca Residence
East Hampton, New York

Goldberg Residence
Manchester, Connecticut

1968

Cooper Residence
Orleans, Massachusetts

Gwathmey, Henderson, and Siegel Architects

Steel Residences I & II
Bridgehampton, New York

Service Building and Heating Plant
State University College at Purchase
Purchase, New York

1969

Dunaway Apartment
New York, New York

Brooklyn Friends School
Brooklyn, New York

Dormitory, Dining and Student Union Facility
State University College at Purchase
Purchase, New York

Gwathmey Siegel Architects

Gwathmey Siegel Architects Offices
New York, New York

1970

Eskilson Residence
Roxbury, Connecticut
(project)

Whig Hall
Princeton University
Princeton, New Jersey

Tolan Residence
Amagansett, New York

1971

New York Apartment
New York, New York

Cogan Residence
East Hampton, New York

Elia-Bash Residence
Califon, New Jersey

1972

Cohn Residence
Amagansett, New York

Whitney Road Housing
Perinton, New York

1973

Gwathmey Barn
Greenwich, Connecticut

Pearl's Restaurant
New York, New York

Sagner Residence
West Orange, New Jersey
(project)

Geffen Residence
California
(project)

St Casmir Housing
Yonkers, New York
(project)

1974

Buettner Residence
Sloatsburg, New York

Transammonia Corporation Offices
New York, New York

Charof Residence
Montauk, New York

Four Seasons Restaurant
Nagoya, Japan
(project)

Kislevitz Residence
Westhampton, New York

Vidal Sassoon Salon
La Costa, California

Vidal Sassoon Salon
New York, New York

Vidal Sassoon Salon
Chicago, Illinois

Vidal Sassoon Salon
Beverly Hills, California

Vidal Sassoon Corporate Offices
Los Angeles, California

1975

Student Apartment Housing
State University College at Purchase
Purchase, New York

Nassau County Art Center
Roslyn, New York
(project)

One Times Square Office Building
New York, New York
(project)

Island Walk Cooperative Housing
Reston, Virginia

Bower and Gardner Law Offices
New York, New York

The Evans Partnership Prototype Office Building

The Evans Partnership Office Building
Piscataway, New Jersey

Unger Apartment
New York, New York

Damson Oil Corporation Office Building
Houston, Texas

US Steakhouse Restaurant
New York, New York

Northpoint Office Building
Houston, Texas

Barber Oil Corporation Offices
New York, New York

1976

East Campus Student Housing and Academic Center
Columbia University
New York, New York

Haupt Residence
Amagansett, New York

Weitz Residence
Quogue, New York

Thomas & Betts Corporation Office Building
Raritan, New Jersey

Benenson Residence
Rye, New York

Swirl Inc. Showroom and Offices
New York, New York

John Weitz Store
Chicago, Illinois

Hyatt Hotel and Casino
Aruba, Antilles
(project)

Swid Apartment I
New York, New York

1977

Poster Originals Ltd Showroom
New York, New York

Garey Shirtmakers Showrooms and Offices
New York, New York

Trammo Petroleum Corporation Offices
New York, New York

Crowley Residence
Greenwich, Connecticut

Geffen Apartment
New York, New York

Belkin Memorial Library
Yeshiva University
New York, New York

Taft Residence
Cincinnati, Ohio

Northgate Housing
Roosevelt Island, New York
(project)

**Lincoln Center for the Performing Arts
Administrative Offices**
New York, New York

FDM Productions Offices
New York, New York

AT&T Office Building
Parsipanny, New Jersey

The Evans Partnership Office Building and Offices
Parsipanny, New Jersey

The Evans Partnership Offices
New York, New York

Gwathmey Siegel & Associates Architects

1978

Amax Petroleum Corporation Office Building
Houston, Texas

Knoll International Showroom and Office Buildings
Boston, Massachusetts

Sycamore Place Elderly Housing
Columbus, Indiana

Pence Street Multi-Family Housing
Columbus, Indiana

Shezan Restaurant
New York, New York

Giorgio Armani, Inc. Showrooms and Offices
New York, New York

1979

Library and Science Building
Westover School
Middlebury, Connecticut

Hines Residence
Martha's Vineyard, Massachusetts
(project)

Triangle Pacific Corporation Office Building
Dallas, Texas

deMenil Residence
Houston, Texas

deMenil Residence
East Hampton, New York

Block Residence
Wilmington, North Carolina
(project)

Einstein Moomjy Showroom
New York, New York

Greenwich Savings Bank
New York, New York

Reliance Group Holdings Inc. Offices
New York, New York

Morton L. Janklow & Associates Offices
New York, New York

Lincoln Center for the Performing Arts Concourse
New York, New York

Viereck Residence
Amagansett, New York

Ally & Gargano Inc. Offices
New York, New York

Desks and Credenza System
Knoll Furniture

Bouchier Westbelt Office Building
Houston, Texas

1980

Bank and Office Building
First City Bank
Houston, Texas

1981

The Evans Partnership Office Building
Montvale, New Jersey

WICK Alumni Center
University of Nebraska
Lincoln, Nebraska

Summit Hotel
New York, New York
(project)

Arango Apartment
New York, New York

Westport Public Library
Westport, Connecticut

deMenil Residence
Santa Monica, California

deMenil Residence
New York, New York
(project)

1982

Gwathmey Siegel & Associates Architects Offices
New York, New York

Steinberg Apartment
New York, New York

Bank and Office Building
Liberty National Bank
Hobbs, New Mexico
(project)

***Solomon R. Guggenheim Museum Addition,
Renovation, and Restoration**
New York, New York
    Associate-in-charge: Jacob Alspector
    Project architects: Pierre Cantacuzene, Gregory
    Karn, Earl Swisher, Steven Forman
    Project team: Paul Aferiat, Patricia Cheung, Nancy
    Clayton, Marc DuBois, David Fratianne, Gerald
    Gendreau, Siamak Hariri, Anthony Iovino, Dirk
    Kramer, Daniel Madlansacay, David Mateer, Jeffrey
    Murphy, Joseph Ruocco, Gary Shoemaker, Irene
    Torroella, Alexandra Villegas, Peter Wiederspahn,
    Ross Wimer, Stephen Yablon

Nassau Park Office Building
West Windsor, New Jersey

IBM Product Center Prototype

IBM Product Center
Albany, New York

The Evans Partnership Office Building
Rutherford, New Jersey

The Evans Partnership Office Building
Paramus, New Jersey

The Evans Partnership Office Building
Parsipanny, New Jersey

Beverly Hills Civic Center
Beverly Hills, California
(Competition)

deMenil Table Series
ICF

Tapestry
V'Soske

1983

Spielberg Apartment
New York, New York

The Evans Partnership Office Building
Piscataway, New Jersey
(project)

*American Museum of the Moving Image
Astoria, New York
    Associate-in-charge: Jacob Alspector
    Project architect: Paul Aferiat
    Project team: Alissa Bucher, Pierre Cantacuzene,
    Stephen Connors, Steven Forman, Timothy Greer,
    Lee Hagen, Rebecca Iovino, Dirk Kramer, Jude
    LeBlanc, Ming Leung, Jay Measley, Carlene Ramus,
    Shalini Taneja

*Knoll International Showroom
Chicago, Illinois
    Associate-in-charge: Jacob Alspector
    Project architect: Paul Aferiat
    Project team: Barry McCormick, Richard Velsor,
    John Petrarca

New York Public Library, Yorkville Branch
New York, New York

Garey Residence
Kent, Connecticut

Swid Apartment II
New York, New York

Bower and Gardner II Law Offices
New York, New York

1984

*John W. Berry Sports Center,
Dartmouth College
Hanover, New Hampshire
    Associate-in-charge: Jacob Alspector
    Project architect: Joseph Ruocco
    Project team: William Gilliland, Siamak Hariri,
    Johannes Kastner, Reese Owens, Peter
    Wiederspahn, Neil Troiano

*College of Agriculture and Life Sciences,
Cornell University
Ithaca, New York
    Associate-in-charge: Thomas Levering
    Project architects: Ronald Ellis, Daniel Rowen
    Project team: Paul Cha, Tom Demetrion, Peter
    Guggenheimer, Joan Jasper, Jim Jorgenson, Thomas
    Lekometros, Jay Levy, Ming Leung, Neil Troiano,
    Wolfram Wohr

Sagner Residence
Essex Fells, New Jersey
(project)

Ogilvy & Mather Offices
Chicago, Illinois

Greenhill School, Lower School Building
Dallas, Texas

Tuxedo Dinnerware
Swid Powell Design

1985

*International Design Centers I & II
Long Island City, New York
    Associates-in-charge: Bruce Donnally, Bruce Nagel
    Associate architect: Stephen Lepp PC Architects &
    Planners

*Basketball Arena and Fieldhouse,
Cornell University
Ithaca, New York
    Associate-in-charge: Peter Guggenheimer
    Project architect: Ronald Ellis
    Project team: E. Jon Frishmen, Ming Leung, Jay
    Levy, Jeffrey Murphy, Guy Oliver, Joan Pierpoline,
    Thomas Savory, Joseph Tanney, Gary Shoemaker,
    Richard Velsor

*IBM Corporation Office Building and Distribution Center
Greensboro, North Carolina
    Associates-in-charge: Thomas Phifer, Richard Velsor
    Project team: Philip Dordai, Malka Friedman, Diane
    Grey, Thomas Lekometros

*East Academic Complex,
Eugenio Maria de Hostos Community College
Bronx, New York
    Associate-in-charge: Jacob Alspector
    Project architect: Thomas Lekometros
    Project team: Jeffrey Bacon, Rustico Bernardo,
    Karen Brenner, Pierre Cantacuzene, Nancy Clayton,
    Thomas Demetrion, Marc DuBois, Ronald Ellis,
    Steven Forman, Peter Franck, Gerald Gendreau,
    Anthony Iovino, Johannes Kastner, Rayme
    Kuniyuki, Ming Leung, Dean Maltz, Paul Mitchell,
    Peter Pawlak, Rebecca Iovino, Joseph Ruocco, Bryce
    Sanders, Thomas Savory, George Selkirk, Lilla
    Smith, Earl Swisher, Joseph Tanney, Dickens van
    der Werff, Richard Velsor, Peter Wiederspahn, Ross
    Wimer, Stephen Yablon

*Morgan Stanley & Co. Inc., World Headquarters
New York, New York
    Associates-in-charge: Gerald Gendreau, Bruce
    Donnally
    Project team: Keith Goich, Sanford Berger, Marc
    DuBois, Dean Maltz, Li Wen

*Center for the Arts,
State University of New York at Buffalo
Amherst, New York
    Associate-in-charge: Dirk Kramer
    Project architect: Philip Dordai
    Project team: Nancy Clayton, Thomas Levering,
    Jeffrey Bacon, Lee Ledbetter, Lilla Smith, Earl
    Swisher
    Associate Architect: Scaffidi and Moore Architects

Financial Benefits Research Group Offices
Roseland, New Jersey

Spielberg Residence
East Hampton, New York

Opel Residence
Shelburne, Vermont

Lexecon Inc. Office Interiors
Chicago, Illinois

International Design Centers III & IV
Long Island City, New York
(project)

1986

Maguire Thomas Partnership Leasing Offices
Dallas, Texas

Steinberg Residence
East Hampton, New York

*Thomas I. Storrs Architecture Building,
University of North Carolina at Charlotte
Charlotte, North Carolina
       Associate-in-charge: Bruce Donnally
       Project architect: Dirk Kramer
       Project team: Jay Measley, Peter Wiederspahn
       Associate architect: The FWA Group

Gimelstob Residence
New Vernon, New Jersey

*Herman Miller Showroom,
International Design Center
Long Island City, New York
       Associate-in-charge: Paul Aferiat
       Project team: Ming Leung, Gerald Gendreau

Birdhouse
The Parrish Art Museum
Southampton, New York

*Stevenson Hall,
Oberlin College
Oberlin, Ohio
       Associate-in-charge: Bruce Donnally
       Project architect: Samuel Anderson
       Project team: Rustico Bernardo, Deborah Cohen,
       Jay Levy, Jeffrey Murphy, Peter Wiederspahn,
       Stephen Yablon

1987

The Georgetown Group Inc. Offices
New York, New York

Bower and Gardner III Law Offices
New York, New York

McCann-Erickson Worldwide World Headquarters Offices
New York, New York

D'Arcy Masius Benton & Bowles Inc. Offices
New York, New York

*SBK Entertainment World Inc. Offices
New York, New York
       Associate-in-charge: Tsun-Kin Tam
       Project architect: Gregory Karn
       Project team: Paul Boardman, Jeffrey Bacon, Philip
       Dordai, Marc DuBois, Dirk Kramer, Thomas
       Lekometros, Jay Levy, Lilla Smith, Malka van
       Bemmelen

*Computer Science Theory Center,
Cornell University
Ithaca, New York
       Associate-in-charge: Thomas Levering
       Project architect: Paul Boardman, Ron Ellis
       Project team: David Biagi, Gregory Karn, Dirk
       Kramer, Joseph Tanney, Malka van Bemmelen

1988

*Oceanfront Residence
Malibu, California
       Associate-in-charge: Gerald Gendreau
       Project architect: Anthony Iovino
       Project team: Nancy Clayton, Gregory Epstein,
       Gregory Karn, Paul Mitchell

*Werner Otto Hall, Busch-Reisinger Museum/
Fine Arts Library Addition to the Fogg Museum
Harvard University
Cambridge, Massachusetts
       Associate-in-charge: Bruce Donnally
       Project architect: Samuel Anderson
       Project team: Johannes Kastner, Rustico Bernardo,
       Joan Jasper, Paul Mitchell

John J. McDonough Museum of Art
Youngstown State University
Youngstown, Ohio

Rosen Townhouses
New York, New York

***Gwathmey Apartment**
New York, New York
      Associate-in-charge: Tsun-Kin Tam

Center for Jewish Life
Duke University
Durham, North Carolina
(project)

Due Restaurant
New York, New York

Chicago Dinnerware
Swid Powell Design

Courtney Vase and Candlestick
Swid Powell Design

1989

***Convention Center and Hotel, EuroDisney**
EuroDisney, SCA
(project)
Marne-la-Vallée, France
      Associate-in-charge: Joseph Ruocco

Leavitt Advertising/Hanover House Offices
Weehawken, New Jersey

Winfrey Apartment
Chicago, Illinois
(project)

***Universal Studios Inc. Divisional Headquarters**
Beverly Hills, California
      Associate-in-charge: Dirk Kramer
      Project architect: Lilla Smith
      Project team: Juan Miro, Joseph Ruocco

Geffen/Salick Office Building
Beverly Hills, California
(project)

***Contemporary Resort Convention Center,
Walt Disney World**
Lake Buena Vista, Florida
      Associate-in-charge: Joseph Ruocco
      Project architect: Keith Howie, Rayme Kuniyuki
      Project team: Edward Arcari, Pat Cheung, Stephen
      DeFossez, David Hendershot, Michelle Kolb,
      Richard Lucas
      Associate architects: Alan Lapidus PC

Koppelman Apartment
New York, New York

Gymnasium/Fieldhouse
State University of New York at Oneonta
Oneonta, New York

Spielberg Guest House
East Hampton, New York

Janklow and Nesbit Literary Agents Offices
New York, New York

SCS Communications Offices
New York, New York

Derby Desk
Knoll Furniture

Knoll Accessories
(project)

1990

***Institute for Human Performance, Rehabilitation
and Biomedical Research,
State University of New York at Syracuse**
Syracuse, New York
      Associate-in-charge: Thomas Levering
      Project architect: Mark Rylander, John Newman,
      Bill Clark
      Project team: Patricia Bosch-Melendez, Sean Flynn,
      Peter Brooks, Lance Hosey, Steve Sudak

Staller Residence
Old Field, New York

Bonnet Creek Golf Clubhouse
Walt Disney World
Lake Buena Vista, Florida

Golf Clubhouse
EuroDisney, SCA
Marne-la-Vallée, France

***Zumikon Residence**
Zumikon, Switzerland
      Associate-in-charge: Bruce Donnally
      Project architect: Nancy Clayton
      Project team: Tom Lewis, Sylvia Becker, Carole
      Iselin
      Associate architect: Pfister & Schiess Architekten

*Taipei Residence
Taipei, Taiwan
(project)
> Associate-in-charge: Jacob Alspector
> Project architect: Gregory Karn
> Project team: Gregory Epstein, Tsun-Kin Tam

*Ronald S. Lauder Foundation Offices
New York, New York
> Associate-in-charge: Tsun-Kin Tam
> Project team: Lilla Smith

Lexecon II Offices
Chicago, Illinois

Anniversary Dinnerware
Swid Powell Design

American Airlines Dinnerware
Swid Powell Design

1991

*Capital Group Inc. Offices
West Los Angeles, California
> Associate-in-charge: Dirk Kramer
> Project architect: Karen Renick
> Project team: Christopher Coe, Peter Brooks, Meta
> Brunzema, Kathleen Byrne, Jay Levy, Lilla Smith

PepsiCo Headquarters Master Plan
Purchase, New York

Sony Entertainment Inc. World Headquarters
New York, New York

***Social Sciences Building and Computer Center,
University of California at San Diego**
La Jolla, California
> Associate-in-charge: Bruce Donnally
> Project architect: Richard Lanier
> Project team: Nancy Clayton, Thomas Lewis
> Associate architect: Brown Gimber Rodriguez Park

***The Science, Industry and Business Library (SIBL),
New York Public Library**
New York, New York
> Associate-in-charge: Jacob Alspector
> Project architect: Earl Swisher
> Project team: Sean Flynn, Karen Brenner, Oana
> Bretcanu, Wendy Burger, Frederico Del Priore,
> Steven Forman, Michael Harshman, Philip
> Henshaw, Mark Hill, Rebecca Iovino, John
> Johnston, James Leet, Thomas Levering, Martin
> Marciano, David Mateer, Cheryl McQueen, Mark
> Montalbano, Jeffrey Poorten, Joseph Rivera,
> Elizabeth Skowronek, Daniel Sullivan

*Stadtportalhäuser
Frankfurt-am-Main, Germany
(competition)
> Associate-in-charge: Jacob Alspector
> Project architect: Gregory Karn

***Master Plan and Three Academic Buildings,
Pitzer College**
Claremont, California
> Associate-in-charge: Gerald Gendreau
> Project architect: Gregory Karn

1992

717 Fifth Avenue Corporate Interior and Lobby
New York, New York

EMI Records Group Office Interiors
New York, New York

*Hilltop Residence
Austin, Texas
> Associate-in-charge: Gustav Rosenlof
> Project architect: Juan Miro
> Project team: Meta Brunzema, Frank Thaler,
> Richard Lucas, Will Meyer, Sean Flynn, Beatrice
> Hunn, Lori Brown

*Nanyang Polytechnic
Singapore
> Associate-in-charge: Joseph Ruocco
> Project architect: Frank Visconti
> Project team: Nelson Benavides, Peter Brooks,
> Gregory Epstein, Mark Hill, Lance Hosey, Joseph
> Hsu, John Hunter, Jay Lampros, Richard Lanier,
> George Liaropoulos, Wei-Li Liu, Greg Luhan,
> Cheryl McQueen, Christine Straw, Frank Thaler
> Associate architect: DP Architects

1993

***Henry Art Gallery Renovation and Addition,
University of Washington**
Seattle, Washington
> Associates-in-charge: Nancy Clayton,
> Bruce Donnally
> Project team: Richard Lucas, Will Meyer
> Associate architect: Loshky, Marquardt & Nesholm

Supercomputer Faculty/Teaching Building
University of California at San Diego
La Jolla, California

*The Museum of Contemporary Art
North Miami, Florida
> Associate-in-charge: Tsun-Kin Tam
> Project architect: Daniel Sullivan
> Project team: Frank Visconti, Gregory Karn
> Associate architect: Gelabert Navia Architects

Citicorp Center Tower, Plaza and Retail Atrium
New York, New York

*San Onofre Residence
Pacific Palisades, California
> Associate-in-charge: Gerald Gendreau
> Project architect: Gregory Epstein
> Project team: Joseph Hsu, Peter Pawlak

***Levitt Center for University Advancement,
University of Iowa**
Iowa City, Iowa
> Associates-in-charge: Nancy Clayton, Bruce
> Donnally
> Project architects: Keith Goich, Will Meyer
> Project team: Victor Rodriguez, John Reed, Patricia
> Brett, Marta Sanders, Meta Bruzema
> Associate architects: Brooks Borg Skiles

Sony Music Entertainment, Inc. Corporate Offices
New York, New York

Barrington Residence
Brentwood, California

*21 International Holdings Inc. Offices
New York, New York
> Associate-in-charge: Tsun-Kin Tam
> Project architect: Jay Levy
> Project team: Daniel Sullivan, Lilla Smith

1994

**Morgan Stanley & Co. Inc., Executive Offices
and Dining Facilities**
New York, New York
> Associates-in-charge: Richard Velsor,
> Thomas Levering
> Project architect: Stephen Yablon
> Project team: Lance Hosey, Peter Brooks, Patricia
> Brett
> Exterior signage design: Gerald Gendreau

Spielberg Apartment
New York, New York

Pomerantz Apartment
New York, New York

*PaceWildenstein Gallery
Beverly Hills, California
> Associate-in-charge: Gerald Gendreau
> Project architect: Tom Lewis, Gregory Karn

1995

*PepsiCo Headquarters Dining Facilities
Purchase, New York
> Associate-in-charge: Thomas Levering
> Project team: Patricia Bosch-Melendez, Sean Flynn,
> David Biagi

Graduate School and University Center
The City University of New York
New York, New York

Medical/Surgical/Oncology Center
The Presbyterian Hospital/Columbia
Presbyterian Medical Center
New York, New York

*Physics Building, Princeton University
Princeton, New Jersey
> Associate-in-charge: Nancy Clayton
> Project architect: Richard Klibschon
> Project team: Peter Brooks, Kang Chang, Christine
> Marriott, David Yum, Peter Juang

Mount Pleasant Blythedale School UFSD
Valhalla, New York

Whig Hall Addition
Princeton University
Princeton, New Jersey

Solomon R. Guggenheim Museum Auditorium Restoration
New York, New York

Punch Production Offices
New York, New York

Winnick Apartment
New York, New York

*Meyer Residence
Malibu, California
> Associate-in-charge: Dirk Kramer
> Project architect: Lilla Smith
> Project team: Christopher Liu, Peter Pawlak

1996

***Baker Library, Graduate School of Business
Administration,
Harvard University**
Cambridge, Massachusetts
      Associate-in-charge: Joseph Ruocco
      Project team: Nelson Benavides, Frank Visconti,
      Sean Flynn
(Competition)

PepsiCo Headquarters Conference Center
Purchase, New York

Geffen Apartment
New York, New York

RSL Foundation Offices
New York, New York

*Casa Vecchia
Bel Air, California
      Associate-in-charge: Gerald Gendreau
      Project architect: Meta Brunzema
      Project team: Daniel Sullivan, John Hunter, Patricia
      Brett, Kang Chang

Saint Vincent's Comprehensive Cancer Center
Salick Health Care Inc.
New York, New York

1997

***University Technology and Learning Complex,
Lawrence Technological University**
Southfield, Michigan
      Associate-in-charge: Gerald Gendreau
      Project architect: Susan Baggs
      Project team: Edward Parker, Daniel Sullivan
      Associate architect: Neumann/Smith Architects

**FSU Library for Information, Technology
and Education (FLITE)**
Ferris State University
Big Rapids, Michigan

**Naismith Memorial Basketball Hall of Fame
and Retail Complex**
Springfield, Massachusetts

Select Bibliography

General Publications

Abercrombie, Stanley. "Gwathmey Siegel: Winner of AIA's 1982 Firm Award: The Art of Architecture at its Most Serious, but also at its Least Mystical." *AIA Journal* (February 1982), pp. 71–80.

"An Abstract Language Made Comprehensible and Comfortable: East Hampton Residence." *AIA Journal* (vol. 73, no. 05, May 1984), pp. 302–313.

"An Interview with Charles Gwathmey." *Pratt Journal of Architecture 1985* (vol. 01, Fall 1985), pp. 26–27.

"Arte Come Itinerario nell'Ignoto/Arts as a Journey into the Unknown." *Architettura: Cronache e Storia* (vol. 37, no. 09, September 1991), pp. 738–739.

"Breaking the Institutional Envelope." *Progressive Architecture* (vol. 73, no. 10, October 1992), pp. 116–117.

Collins, Brad & Kasprowicz, Diane (eds). *Gwathmey Siegel: Buildings and Projects 1982–1992.* New York: Rizzoli International Publications, 1993. (A comprehensive monograph from 1982–1992)

"Conversa com Charles Gwathmey (Interview)." *Projecto* (no. 125, September 1989), p. 24.

"Entrevista: Charles Gwathmey (Interview)." *Arquitectura* (vol. 70, no. 277, March–April 1989), pp. 116–132.

"Gwathmey Siegel & Associates Architects." *Architectural Digest* (vol. 47, no. 05, May 1990), pp. 206–213, 276.

"Gwathmey Siegel at 25: The Sky's the Limit." *Interiors* (vol. 13, no. 09, September 1993), pp. 55–83.

"Gwathmey Siegel" *Häuser* (December 1997), pp. 51–62.

"Gwathmey, Eisenman, Graves, Stern: Guest Appearances." *Iowa Architect* (vol. 40, no. 03, Fall 1991), pp. 10–15.

"Hall of Fame: Gwathmey Siegel & Associates." *Interior Design* (December 1988).

"Hot Spots: Bold New Design Mixes for Four Fashionable Spots." *Interiors* (vol. 148, no. 05, December 1988), p. 16.

"Interview with Charles Gwathmey." *Il Progetto 2* (January 1997), pp. 18–27.

"Into the Black Box." *Design Quarterly* (no. 156, Summer 1992), pp. 6–9.

Jacobs, Jay. "The Master Builder." *Pennsylvania Gazette* (March 1992), pp. 31–36.

"Les Cendres de Jefferson." *L'Architecture d'Aujourd'hui* (August–September 1976), pp. 53–72.

"Office Furniture: Round Table." *Record Interiors* (February 1982).

"Only Connect." *Building Design* (no. 150, September 27, 1991), p. 2.

"A Section Through the Thinking of Gwathmey Siegel Architects." *Architectural Record* (vol. 166, no. 04, September 1979), pp. 91–102.

"Special Feature: Gwathmey Siegel & Associates Architects." *A+U* (no. 04, April 1989), pp. 39–41.

"The 'A' List for the Baby Boom." *Time* (November 10, 1986).

"Un Architettura per il Design/ Architecture for Design." *l'Arca* (no. 09, September 1987), pp. 30–37.

Vogel, Carol. "Seeing New York City Through the Eyes of Its Architects." *New York Times* (October 30, 1987), p. C27.

Publications on Specific Projects

"1585 Broadway, Solomon Equities Inc., New York, USA." *A+U* (no. 04, April 1989), pp. 128–129. (Morgan Stanley & Co. Inc. World Headquarters)

A+U (Japan, June 1995), pp. 102–115. (Zumikon Residence)

Abercombie, Stanley & Dundes, Lester. *Corporate Interiors.* New York: Retail Reporting Corporation, 1997, pp. 82–83. (21 International Holdings Inc. Headquarters; Capital Group Inc. Offices; Ronald S. Lauder Foundation Offices)

Abercrombie, Stanley. "Does New York Need a Design Center?" *Interior Design* (July 1983), pp. 176–177. (International Design Center)

Abercrombie, Stanley. "How to Succeed in Business: Gwathmey Siegel Headquarters for Morgan Stanley Stand Confidently at the Edge of Times Square." *Interior Design* (September 1996), pp. 126–134. (Morgan Stanley & Co. Inc. World Headquarters)

"Academics: High-rise Residences." *Process Architecture* (no. 64, January 1986), pp. 133–153. (Spielberg Apartment One)

Adaptive Re-use and Commercial Remodeling Winner: Gwathmey Siegel & Associates Create the Unique International Design Center." *Interiors* (vol. 146, no. 06, January 1987), pp. 186–187. (International Design Center)

"Adaptive Re-use of Buildings." *Southeast Asia Building* (November 1996), pp. 16–24. (American Museum of the Moving Image; Henry Art Gallery Renovation and Addition; Science, Industry and Business Library; Solomon R. Guggenheim Museum Addition, Renovation, and Restoration)

"Additions to the Guggenheim and Whitney Museums." *International Journal of Museum Management and Curatorship* (March 1986), pp. 92–95. (Solomon R. Guggenheim Museum Addition, Renovation, and Restoration)

"Administration, Academic Building, School of Agriculture, Cornell University, Ithaca, New York, USA." *A+U* (no. 04, April 1989), pp. 108–109. (College of Agriculture and Life Sciences)

American Houses Now. New York: Universe Publications/Rizzoli International Publications, 1997. (Pacific Palisades Residence)

"Ampliamenti alla Harvard University di Cambridge, Mass." *L'Industria delle Construzioni* (vol. 27, no. 256, February 1993), pp. 36–43. (Werner Otto Hall, Busch-Reisinger Museum)

"An International Design Center Planned for New York." *Interior Design* (April 1983), p. 86. (International Design Center)

Anderson, Kurt. "Finally Doing Right by Wright." *Time* (July 6, 1992), pp. 64–65. (Solomon R. Guggenheim Museum Addition, Renovation, and Restoration)

Anderson, Kurt. "Look Mickey, No Kitsch! Disney Has Become the World's Foremost Patron of High–profile Architecture." *Time* (July 29, 1991), p. 69. (Contemporary Resort Convention Center, Walt Disney World)

ANY Magazine (January 1998). (Solomon R. Guggenheim Museum Addition, Renovation, and Restoration)

Architectural Digest: Das Internationale Wohnmagazin. (1997). (Pacific Palisades Residence)

"Architectural Showcase." *Athletic Business* (June 1990). (Basketball Arena and Fieldhouse)

Architecture (July 1995), p. 41. (Nanyang Polytechnic)

Architektur & Wohnen (1997). (Henry Art Gallery Renovation and Addition)

"Astoria Studio Revives Film Era in New York." *New York Times* (August 3, 1983), p. C17. (American Museum of the Moving Image)

"At Trump Tower: A New York Co-op Apartment by Gwathmey Siegel & Associates Architects." *Interior Design* (April 1986), pp. 250–257. (Spielberg Apartment One)

"Avant Guardians: Gwathmey Siegel's Guggenheim Addition." *Building Stone Magazine* (November–December 1986), pp. 24–35. (Solomon R. Guggenheim Museum Addition, Renovation, and Restoration)

"Back to the Further." *Interiors* (vol. 151, no. 07, July 1992), pp. 22–24, 82. (Solomon R. Guggenheim Museum Addition, Renovation, and Restoration)

Bonetti, David. "Harvard's Multilingual Concerto: New Museum Annex a Triumphant Linking of Styles." *San Francisco Examiner* (February 7, 1992). (Werner Otto Hall, Busch-Reisinger Museum; Solomon R. Guggenheim Museum Addition, Renovation, and Restoration)

"Born Again: A Masterpiece Saved or Compromised?" *Architectural Record* (October 1992), pp. 100–113. (Solomon R. Guggenheim Museum Addition, Renovation, and Restoration)

Burnett, Linda. "Store of Knowledge." *Contract Design* (June 6, 1997), pp 66–71. (Science, Industry and Business Library)

Campbell, Robert. "Why It Works as Architecture: Modernism with Good Manners." *Boston Globe* (September 22, 1991). (Werner Otto Hall, Busch-Reisinger Museum)

Carter, Brian (ed.). *International Architecture Yearbook*. Melbourne, Australia: The Images Publishing Group, 1995, pp. 184–189. (Zumikon Residence)

"Charles Gwathmey: University at Buffalo Fine Arts Center (Interview)." *Intersight* (vol. 01, 1990), pp. 36–43. (Center for the Arts, State University of New York at Buffalo)

"Check out Business Help at Two Upgraded Libraries." *Crain's New York Business* (May 13, 1996). (Science, Industry and Business Library)

Cohen, Edie Lee. "Gwathmey Siegel's 21 Holding." *Interior Design* (May 1995). (21 International Holdings Inc. Headquarters)

Cohen, Edie Lee. "Gwathmey Siegel: The Surprisingly Human-Scaled Offices of Ronald S. Lauder." *Interior Design* (vol. 73, no. 10, August–September 1992), pp. 116–117. (Ronald S. Lauder Foundation Offices)

Cohen, Mark Francis. "Hostos Theater: New and Hot." *New York Times* (December 17, 1995), p. 10. (East Academic Complex, Eugenio Maria de Hostos Community College)

Colford, Paul D. "Watch This: The Material Culture of Motion Pictures and Television Finds a Home in Astoria." *Newsday* (July 5, 1988), pp. 4, 11. (American Museum of the Moving Image)

Collins, Brad (ed). *Zumikon Residence*. New York: The Monacelli Press, 1996. (Zumikon Residence)

"Commentary: Adding to Icons." *Progressive Architecture* (no. 06, June 1990), pp. 124–125. (Solomon R. Guggenheim Museum Addition, Renovation, and Restoration)

"Construction Begins in August of the COCA/Center of Contemporary Art." *Sun Post* (July 14, 1994). (Museum of Contemporary Art)

"Contextual Modernism, 3 New Cornell University Buildings." *AIA Journal* (vol. 80, no. 01, January 1991), pp. 38–47. (Basketball Arena and Fieldhouse; College of Agriculture and Life Sciences; Computer Science Theory Center)

Cooper, Jerry. "SBK: Recent Work by Gwathmey Siegel." *Interior Design* (vol. 60, no. 03, February 1989), pp. 198–207. (SBK Entertainment World Inc. Offices)

Cormier, Lesli Humm. "Muses, Museums and Artistic Intent: The New Building for the Busch-Reisinger Museum." *Art New England* (April 1989), pp. 6–7. (Werner Otto Hall, Busch-Reisinger Museum; Solomon R. Guggenheim Museum Addition, Renovation, and Restoration)

"Dartmouth College, John W. Berry Sports Center, Hanover, New Hampshire." *Architectural Portfolio* (November 1990), pp. 268–269. (John W. Berry Sports Center)

"Das Neue Guggenheim Museum, New York." *Bauwelt* (vol. 83, no. 27, July 17, 1992), pp. 1559–1560. (Solomon R. Guggenheim Museum Addition, Renovation, and Restoration)

Dean, Andrea Oppenheimer. "Renewing our Modern Legacy." *Architecture* (November 1990), p. 65. (Solomon R. Guggenheim Museum Addition, Renovation, and Restoration; Werner Otto Hall, Busch-Reisinger Museum)

"Design Leaders Rally around New York's International Design Center." *Interiors* (December 1983). (International Design Center)

"Design Trends." *Interiors* (June 1988), pp. 162–167. (Herman Miller Showroom)

Dietsch, Deborah K. "Art and Industry." *Architectural Record* (May 1989), pp. 109–110, 116–121. (American Museum of the Moving Image)

Dietsch, Deborah K. "Spatial Effects: Trump Tower Apartment, New York City, Gwathmey Siegel & Associates." *Architectural Record* (vol. 170, no. 03, mid-September 1985), pp. 162–169. (Spielberg Apartment One)

Dimitriu, Livio. *New York Architects 3.* New York: Urban Studies and Architecture Group, 1990, pp. 105–113. (Werner Otto Hall, Busch-Reisinger Museum)

"Dinner at the Home Page Restaurant." *Metropolis* (March 1996), p. 44. (Science, Industry and Business Library)

"Doing Right by Wright." *New York Magazine* (December 2, 1985), pp. 132–134. (Solomon R. Guggenheim Museum Addition, Renovation, and Restoration)

"Double Feature: Two Museums of the Moving Image." *Architectural Record* (vol. 177, no. 06, May 1989), pp. 109–121. (American Museum of the Moving Image)

Dugdale, Juanita. "Wayfinding Takes a Detour." *Print* (July–August 1997), pp. 58–67. (Science, Industry and Business Library)

Duhart, Olympia. "Ground-breaking Set for N. Miami Museum." *Miami Herland* (December 9, 1993). (Museum of Contemporary Art)

Dunlope, Beth. "Architecture: South Florida Takes Tentative Steps toward Becoming a World-class Region." *Miami Herald* (December 26, 1993). (Museum of Contemporary Art)

Dunlope, Beth. "Museum Plan Rich with Subtleties, Allusions." *Miami Herald* (December 12, 1993). (Museum of Contemporary Art)

"East Academic Complex, Hostos Community College, Bronx, New York, USA." *A+U* (no. 04, April 1989), pp. 118–119. (East Academic Complex, Eugenio Maria de Hostos Community College)

"El Guggenheim Re-figurado/The Guggenheim Re-figured." *Arquitectura* (vol. 01, July 1992), pp. 112–120. (Solomon R. Guggenheim Museum Addition, Renovation, and Restoration)

"Environmental Graphic Design Awards." *How* (August 1997), p. 44. (Science, Industry and Business Library)

"Erweiterung des Solomon R. Guggenheim Museums." *Bauwelt* (vol. 83, no. 6–7, February 14, 1992), pp. 310–311. (Solomon R. Guggenheim Museum Addition, Renovation, and Restoration)

"A Far Better Thing: The Guggenheim and Whitney Redesign Their Expansion Schemes." *Architectural Record* (vol. 175, no. 04, April 1987). (Solomon R. Guggenheim Museum Addition, Renovation, and Restoration)

Finke, Gail Deibler. "Timeless Elegance." *VM+SD* (December 1996), pp. 68–69. (Science, Industry and Business Library)

Fischer, Holger. "Neuer Glanz hinter Fabrikmauern." *DB/Deutsche Bauzeitung* (September 1989), p. 41. (International Design Center)

"Forms of Attachment: Addition to Modern American Monuments." *Lotus International* (no. 72, 1992), pp. 90–95. (Solomon R. Guggenheim Museum Addition, Renovation, and Restoration)

Frampton, Kenneth. "Gwathmey Siegel Works." *A+U* (special issue, January 1993), pp. 72–101. (Solomon R. Guggenheim Museum Addition, Renovation, and Restoration; Werner Otto Hall, Busch-Reisinger Museum)

Fujii, Wayne N.T. *GA Houses 34* (Tokyo, March 1992), pp. 22–23. (Zumikon Residence)

GA Houses 48 (Tokyo, March 1996), pp 44–47 (Hilltop Residence), 40–43 (Malibu Residence), 48–51 (Pacific Palisades Residence).

Gandee, Charles K. "A Bridge Too Far?" *Architectural Record* (June 1986), pp. 144–153. (International Design Center)

Gandee, Charles. "Special Feature: Gwathmey Siegel & Associates." *A+U* (April 1989), pp. 39–134. (American Museum of the Moving Image; IBM Corporation Office Building and Distribution Center; John W. Berry Sports Center)

Giovannini, Joseph. "Architecture Gwathmey Siegel: A Modernist Villa Set into the Hills near Zurich." *Architectural Digest* (November 1996), pp. 144–152. (Zumikon Residence)

Giovannini, Joseph. "Science Library Opens in New York City." *Architecture* (June 1996). (Science, Industry and Business Library)

Goldberger, Paul. "Grandeur and Modernity in a New Library." *New York Times* (April 24 1996). (Science, Industry and Business Library)

Goldberger, Paul. "In Times Square Dignity by Day, Glitter by Night." *New York Times* (February 10, 1991). (Morgan Stanley & Co. Inc. World Headquarters)

Goldberger, Paul. "When Art Talks Back to Buildings, We Listen." *New York Times* (December 1, 1996), p. H49. (Solomon R. Guggenheim Museum Addition, Renovation, and Restoration)

Gonzalez, David. "Excavating a Monument to Foresight." *New York Times* (November 13, 1996). (Science, Industry and Business Library)

"Goodbye Room 227, Hello SIBL: Library Renewal." *Metropolis* (March 1996), p. 49. (Science, Industry and Business Library)

Goodman, Wendy. "Gwathmey on the Rise." *Harper's Bazaar* (July 1995), pp. 119–124. (Solomon R. Guggenheim Museum Addition, Renovation, and Restoration)

Graaf, Vera. "Ein moderner Schrein für deutsche Kunst." *Feuilleton* (September 30, 1991). (Werner Otto Hall, Busch-Reisinger Museum)

"The Great Museum Debate: Gwathmey Siegel & Associates Discuss Proposed Guggenheim Addition." *Oculus,* (vol. 47, no. 08, April 1986), pp. 4–5,14–16. (Solomon R. Guggenheim Museum Addition, Renovation, and Restoration)

Griffith, Victoria. "NY Learns There's More to Books." *Financial Times* (June 10, 1996). (Science, Industry and Business Library)

"The Guggenheim Addition." *Oculus* (vol. 47, no. 06, February 1986), pp. 12–15. (Solomon R. Guggenheim Museum Addition, Renovation, and Restoration)

"Guggenheim Dilemma." *Building Design* (September 12, 1986), pp. 30–36. (Solomon R. Guggenheim Museum Addition, Renovation, and Restoration)

"Guggenheim Expansion Under Ground." *Oculus* (November 1986). (Solomon R. Guggenheim Museum Addition, Renovation, and Restoration)

"The Guggenheim Museum Addition & Werner Otto Hall." *A+U* (no. 268, January 1993), pp. 72–101. (Solomon R. Guggenheim Museum Addition, Renovation, and Restoration; Werner Otto Hall, Busch-Reisinger Museum)

"The Guggenheim Museum Addition." *A+U* (no. 04, April 1989), pp. 124–125. (Solomon R. Guggenheim Museum Addition, Renovation, and Restoration)

"The Guggenheim Museum Announces Revised Expansion Plans." *Oculus* (vol. 146, no. 11, April 1987), p. 224. (Solomon R. Guggenheim Museum Addition, Renovation, and Restoration)

"Guggenheim Reopens, Expanded and Renovated." *Progressive Architecture* (vol. 73, no. 08, August 1992), pp. 13–14. (Solomon R. Guggenheim Museum Addition, Renovation, and Restoration)

"Guggenheim Revision." *Progressive Architecture* (vol. 68, no. 03, March 1987), pp. 41, 43. (Solomon R. Guggenheim Museum Addition, Renovation, and Restoration)

"Guggenheim Unveils Modified Gwathmey Siegel Addition." *Architecture: AIA Journal* (vol. 76, no. 03, March 1987), pp. 40–42. (Solomon R. Guggenheim Museum Addition, Renovation, and Restoration)

"Guggenheim-Museum in New York." *Baumeister* (vol. 89, no. 09, September 1992), pp. 26–29. (Solomon R. Guggenheim Museum Addition, Renovation, and Restoration)

"Guggenheim: Wright or Wrong." *Metropolis* (vol. 06, no. 03, October 1986), pp. 32–33. (Solomon R. Guggenheim Museum Addition, Renovation, and Restoration)

Gunts, Edward. "Contextual Modernism." *Architecture Magazine* (January 1991). (Basketball Arena and Fieldhouse; College of Agriculture and Life Sciences; Computer Science Theory Center)

Guzzoni, Edoardo. "Nuovo Centro Sportive del Dartmouth College, Hanover/New Hampshire." *Domus* (no. 703, March 1989), pp. 46–51. (Basketball Arena and Fieldhouse)

"Gwathmey & Siegel a New York: L'Amplicamento." *Abitare* (no. 310, September 1992), pp. 203–209, 274. (Solomon R. Guggenheim Museum Addition, Renovation, and Restoration)

"Gwathmey Experiments with Luminous Ceiling." *Architectural Lighting* (May 1989). (SBK Entertainment World Inc. Offices)

"The Gwathmey House and Studio, 1967, Amagansett, New York, USA." *Toshi-Jutaku Process Architecture* (July 1983), pp. 96–99. (Gwathmey Apartment)

"Gwathmey Siegel & Associates Architects Stretch the Language of Modernism to New Limits in Offices for Lexecon and Maguire/Thomas." *Interiors* (vol. 147, no. 04, November 1987), pp. 144–153. (Lexecon II)

"Gwathmey Siegel & Associates, International Design Center New York." *Domus* (February 1988), pp. 46–56. (International Design Center)

"Gwathmey Siegel: Form Follows Function in a Fifth Avenue Apartment." *Architectural Digest* (vol. 45, no. 08, August 1988), pp. 74–75. (Gwathmey Apartment)

Hackett, Regina. "Oh, Henry." *Seattle Post Intelligencer* (April 3, 1997), pp. C1–C4. (Henry Art Gallery Renovation and Addition)

"Harvard's Tough Tack: Putting an Addition on an Addition." *Museum News* (vol. 76, no. 03, May–June 1989), pp. 18–19. (Werner Otto Hall, Busch-Reisinger Museum)

Henderson, Justin. *Museum Architecture*. Seattle: Rockport Publishers, 1998. (Henry Art Gallery Renovation and Addition)

"The Henry in Context." *Arcade* (vol. XV, no. 3, Spring 1997), pp. 36–37. (Henry Art Gallery Renovation and Addition)

Hightower, Marvin. "New Home for Busch-Reisinger To Open." *Harvard University Gazette* (September 20, 1991). (Werner Otto Hall, Busch-Reisinger Museum)

Holusha, John. "New York Library Nears Start on Science Center." *New York Times* (April 6, 1993), p. D2. (Science, Industry and Business Library)

Il Progetto (1997). (Nanyang Polytechnic; Pacific Palisades Residence; Solomon R. Guggenheim Museum Addition, Renovation, and Restoration; Zumikon Residence)

"In Queens, a Design Center that Lives up to Its Name: Design Center Makes an Imprint." *New York Times* (Sunday, January 10, 1988), p. 35. (International Design Center)

International Architecture Yearbook. Melbourne, Australia: The Images Publishing Group, 1997, pp. 188–191. (Science, Industry and Business Library)

"International Design Center, New Long Island City Development." *Contract* (May 1983), p. 86. (International Design Center)

"International Design Center, New York." *Oculus* (vol. 47, no. 03, November 1985). (International Design Center)

Jessup, Lynn. "The Men with a Plan for Summit Green." *Life & Leisure* (June 22, 1986). (IBM Corporation Office Building and Distribution Center)

Jodidio, Philip. "Contemporary American Architects." *Taschen* (1993), pp. 74–81. (Contemporary Resort Convention Center, Walt Disney World; Solomon R. Guggenheim Museum Addition, Renovation, and Restoration; Taipei Residence)

Johnson, Ken. "Starship Guggenheim." *Art in America* (July 1992), pp. 106–119. (Solomon R. Guggenheim Museum Addition, Renovation, and Restoration)

Kimmelman, Michael. "Ambitious Miami Reaches for a Place in the Sun." *New York Times* (March 31, 1996). (Museum of Contemporary Art)

"Knoll: Gwathmey Siegel Provide a Quiet but Not Mute Backdrop." *Interior Design* (vol. 57, no. 09, September 1986). (Knoll International Showroom)

Kroloff, Reed. "Campus Fragments." *Architecture Magazine* (September 1997), pp. 120–127. (Henry Art Gallery Renovation and Addition)

"L'Ampliamento del Solomon R. Guggenheim Museum di Gwathmey Siegel/Addition to the Solomon R. Guggenheim Museum in New York." *Casabella* (vol. 594, October 1992), pp. 4–17, 68–70, cover. (Solomon R. Guggenheim Museum Addition, Renovation, and Restoration)

"L'Art de ce Siècle." *Connaissance des Arts* (no. 485–486, July–August 1992, pp. 36–43. (Solomon R. Guggenheim Museum Addition, Renovation, and Restoration)

"La Rinnovata Henry Art Gallery." *l'Arca* (June 1997), p. 102. (Henry Art Gallery Renovation and Addition)

"La Saga des Musées Guggenheim." *Architecture Intérieure Crée* (no. 250, October 1992), pp. XLII–XLIII. (Solomon R. Guggenheim Museum Addition, Renovation, and Restoration)

Larson, Kay. "The Wright Stuff." *New York Magazine* (June 1, 1992). (Solomon R. Guggenheim Museum Addition, Renovation, and Restoration)

"Law: Substantial Completion." *Progressive Architecture* (vol. 74, no. 01, January 1993), p. 33. (Solomon R. Guggenheim Museum Addition, Renovation, and Restoration)

"Leaving Wright Enough Alone." *Architectural Record* (vol. 174, no. 03, March 1986), pp. 79, 81–83. (Solomon R. Guggenheim Museum Addition, Renovation, and Restoration)

Levinson, Nancy. "Sleek New Home for the Busch-Reisinger: A Harvard Museum Known for German Art Finds." *Christian Science Monitor* (October 29, 1991). (Werner Otto Hall, Busch-Reisinger Museum)

Lovine, Juile V. "State of the Art Gallery: LA goes SoHo." *New York Times Magazine* (December 10, 1995). (PaceWildenstein Art Gallery)

Mallis, Fern. "Una Casa Per il Design." *Abitare* (January–February 1986). (International Design Center)

Mannes, George. "The Library of Tomorrow is here Today." *Daily News* (May 5, 1996). (Science, Industry and Business Library)

May, Vernon. "Revealing Wright." *Progressive Architecture* (April 1989). (Solomon R. Guggenheim Museum Addition, Renovation, and Restoration)

Mays, Vernon. "Beyond Convention." *Architecture Magazine* (January 1992). (Contemporary Resort Convention Center, Walt Disney World)

McGuigan, Cathleen. "Do the Wright Thing." *Newsweek* (June 29, 1992), pp. 58–62. (Solomon R. Guggenheim Museum Addition, Renovation, and Restoration)

Merkel, Jane. "College Redesign Promises To Be Instructive as well as Functional." *Cincinnati Enquirer* (February 17, 1988), p. G9. (College of Agriculture and Life Sciences)

Merlot, Michel (ed.). *Nouvelles Alexandries: Les Grands Chantiers de Bibliothèques dans le Monde*. Paris: Collection Bibliothèques, Editions du Cercle de la Librairie, 1996, pp. 232–259. (Science, Industry and Business Library)

Metz, Tracy. "Living with Art." *Architectural Record* (April 1995). (Zumikon Residence)

"Miracle on Madison." *New York Times* (May 11, 1996). (Science, Industry and Business Library)

"Modern Mediator: Werner Otto Hall, Harvard University, Cambridge Massachusetts, Gwathmey Siegel & Associates Architects." *Architecture* (vol. 80, no. 11, November 1991). (Werner Otto Hall, Busch-Reisinger Museum)

Moonan, Wendy. "The Maker's Mark." *House & Garden* (vol. 116, no. 9, September 1997), pp. 166–177. (Pacific Palisades Residence)

"Movies in Motion: At a New Museum Devoted to Film and Television the Visitor Becomes as Active as the Figures on the Screen." *House & Garden* (vol. 160, no. 06, June 1988), pp. 26–27. (American Museum of the Moving Image)

"Multipurpose Fieldhouse, Cornell University, Ithaca, New York, USA." *A+U* (April 1989), pp. 39–134. (Basketball Arena and Fieldhouse)

Muschamp, Herbert. "A City of Glitter and Ashes." *New York Times* (March 10, 1996). (Museum of Contemporary Art)

"Museos Crecederos: El Guggenheim y el Mass Moca." *Arquitectura Viva* (no. 16, January–February 1991), pp. 8–11. (College of Agriculture and Life Sciences)

"Museu Guggenheim, Nova York, Estados Unidos." *Projeto* (vol. 13, no. 03, April 1993), pp. 36–42. (Solomon R. Guggenheim Museum Addition, Renovation, and Restoration)

"Museum Piece: Joseph Giovannini on Architecture." *Artforum* (vol. 25, no. 09, May 1987), pp. 2–5. (Solomon R. Guggenheim Museum Addition, Renovation, and Restoration)

"Nanyang Polytechnic's Permanent Campus." *Asian Building and Construction* (vol. 6, no. 3), pp. 57–62. (Nanyang Polytechnic)

Nasater, Judith. "Public Access." *Interior Design* (June 1996). (Science, Industry and Business Library)

Nemser, Rebecca. "Seeing the Light." *Boston Phoenix* (September 27, 1991). (Werner Otto Hall, Busch-Reisinger Museum)

"Neuer Glanz Hinter Fabrikmauern: Das International Design Center, New York." *Deutsche Bauzeitung* (vol. 59, no. 14, September 1988), pp. 222–227. (International Design Center)

"New York's IDC Opening." *Progressive Architecture* (vol. 66, no. 11, November 1985), p. 36. (International Design Center)

"New York: L'Ampliamento del Guggenheim Museum." *Domus* (no. 671, April 1986), pp. 1–3. (Solomon R. Guggenheim Museum Addition, Renovation, and Restoration)

"North Campus Dining Facility, Oberlin College, Oberlin, Ohio, USA." *A+U* (no. 04, April 1989), pp. 114–115. (Stevenson Hall, Oberlin College)

"Old and New: Gwathmey Siegel's Guggenheim Addition Draws Mixed Reactions." *AIA Journal* (December 1985). (Solomon R. Guggenheim Museum Addition, Renovation, and Restoration)

"On Center: The IDCNY Complex by Gwathmey Siegel & Associates." *Interiors* (vol. 150, no. 14, September 1991), pp. 88–89. (International Design Center)

"Onward and Upward in the South Bronx, Hostos Community College." *Architectural Record* (vol. 175, no. 12, October 1987), p. 71. (East Academic Complex, Eugenio Maria de Hostos Community College)

Paganelli, Carlo. "Negativo e Positivo: Henry Art Gallery, Seattle." *l'Arca* (June 1997), pp. 54–57. (Henry Art Gallery Renovation and Addition)

Pastier, John. "Enlightened Spaces." *Seattle Weekly* (April 16, 1997), pp. 24–27. (Henry Art Gallery Renovation and Addition)

Pastore, Daniela. "La Casa Unifamiliare nella Cultura Americana: Gwathmey & Siegel, Poetica della Nostalgia." *Controspazio* (June 1994), pp. 46–51. (Zumikon Residence)

Pittel, Christin. "Finally: The Guggenheim as Wright Conceived." *House Beautiful* (June 1992), pp. 83–88. (Solomon R. Guggenheim Museum Addition, Renovation, and Restoration)

Powell, Kenneth. "The Famous Five." *Perspectives on Architecture* (February–March 1997), pp. 34–41. (Zumikon Residence)

"Proposed Guggenheim Addition Debate at Municipal Hearing." *AIA Journal* (vol. 75, no. 08, August 1986), pp. 10–12. (Solomon R. Guggenheim Museum Addition, Renovation, and Restoration)

"Queens Site To Be Converted into an International Design Center." *New York Times* (March 10, 1983), p. C1. (International Design Center)

"The Quest Whitney?" *Friends of Kebyar* (vol. 4/2, no. 28, March–April), pp. 4–5. (Solomon R. Guggenheim Museum Addition, Renovation, and Restoration)

Riera Ojeda, Oscar & Guerra, Lucas H. (eds). *Hyper-Realistic: Computer Generated Architectural Renderings.* Massachusetts: Rockport Publishers, 1996, pp. 110–111. (Nanyang Polytechnic; Science, Industry and Business Library)

Riera Ojeda, Oscar (ed.). *The New American House.* New York: Whitney Library of Design, 1995, pp. 252–261. (Zumikon Residence)

Riera Ojeda, Oscar (ed.) *The New American House II.* New York: Whitney Library of Design, 1997. (Pacific Palisades Residence)

Riera Ojeda, Oscar (ed.). *Ten Houses: Gwathmey Siegel.* Massachusetts: Rockport Publishers, 1995. (Hilltop Residence; Oceanfront Residence; Taipei Residence; Zumikon Residence)

"Rooms with a Point of View." *New York Times Magazine* (October 20, 1991). (Gwathmey Apartment)

"The Ruin of the Guggenheim." *Architettura* (vol. 38, no. 12, December 1991), p. 887. (Solomon R. Guggenheim Museum Addition, Renovation, and Restoration)

Russell, Beverly. "Gwathmey Siegel at 25: The Sky's the Limit." *Interiors* (September 1993). (American Museum of the Moving Image; Morgan Stanley & Co. Inc. World Headquarters; Ronald S. Lauder Foundation Offices; Science, Industry and Business Library; Capital Group Inc. Offices; Universal Studios Inc. Divisional Headquarters)

Sachner, Paul M. "Face Value." *Architectural Record* (October 1988), pp. 82–87. (IBM Corporation Office Building and Distribution Center)

Salisbury, Wilma. "Campus Charmer." *Plain Dealer Magazine* (January 3, 1986), pp. 16, 17. (Stevenson Hall, Oberlin College)

"SBK: Recent Work by Gwathmey Siegel." *Interior Design* (vol. 60, no. 03, February 1989), pp. 198–207. (SBK Entertainment World Inc. Offices)

Schmertz, Mildred F. "Architecture for the Arts: Wright Revamped." *Architecture Magazine* (August 1992). (Solomon R. Guggenheim Museum Addition, Renovation, and Restoration)

"Science, Industry and Business Library Renaissance and Revival." *Metalworks* (April 1996), pp. 1–3. (Science, Industry and Business Library)

"Sede della IBM a Greensboro/IBM Headquarters in Greensboro, N.C." *L'Industria delle Construzioni* (July–August 1989). (IBM Corporation Office Building and Distribution Center)

Selden, Brigitte. "Ein Haus wie ein Bergdorf." *Privé: Das Wohnmagazin* (May 1994), pp. 60–67. (Zumikon Residence)

"Something Old, Something New and Something Added." *Museum News* (vol. 66, no. 04, December 1988), pp. 16–18. (Solomon R. Guggenheim Museum Addition, Renovation, and Restoration; Werner Otto Hall, Busch-Reisinger Museum)

Southeast Asia Building (May 1997), p. 82. (Nanyang Polytechnic)

Spiegel, Joseph. "Renovating an All-Wright Design." *Sound & Communications* (October 1996), pp. 58–61. (Solomon R. Guggenheim Museum Addition, Renovation, and Restoration)

Stein, Karen D. "Next Century's Library— Today." *Architectural Record* (September 1996), pp. 84–92. (Science, Industry and Business Library)

Stucchi, Silvano. "Casa Unfamiliare a Zumicon, Zurigo." *L'Industria delle Construzioni* (no. 296, June 1996), pp. 20–27. (Zumikon Residence)

Stuchin, Marcie. *Waterside Homes* (1997). (Pacific Palisades Residence)

Temin, Christine. "Busch is Back." *Boston Globe* (September 22, 1991). (Werner Otto Hall, Busch-Reisinger Museum)

Temin, Christine. "Seattle's Art of the Moment: A Museum Building Boom Shows Off the City's Financial and Artistic Wealth." *Boston Sunday Globe* (May 11, 1997). (Henry Art Gallery Renovation and Addition)

"Theater Art and Fine Art Building, State University of New York at Buffalo, Amherst, New York, USA." *A+U* (April 1989), pp. 120–121. (Center for the Arts, State University of New York at Buffalo)

"The Theory Center, Cornell University, Ithaca, New York, USA." *A+U* (April 1989), pp. 112–113. (Computer Science Theory Center)

Truppin, Andrea. "Design for Design." *Interiors* (July 1996). (International Design Center)

"Twin Shrines to the Silver Screen." *Time* (September 26, 1988), p. 96. (American Museum of the Moving Image)

"Two Proposals for the 90's: Whitney and Guggenheim Museums Extensions, New York." *Studio International* (vol. 199, no. 1014, September 1986), pp. 4–11. (Solomon R. Guggenheim Museum Addition, Renovation, and Restoration)

"Un Prestigieux Centre International d'Exposition." *Club Maison* (September 1983). (International Design Center)

"Una Casa Per Il Design: IDCNY International Design Center New York." *Abitare* (1985). (International Design Center)

Vercelloni, Matteo & San Pietro, Silvio (eds). *Urban Interiors in New York.* New York: Edizione L'Archivolto, 1996, pp. 78–87. (Gwathmey Apartment)

Viladas, Pilar. "Soft Sell." *Progressive Architecture* (March 1988). (Herman Miller Showroom)

Vitta, Maurizio. "Un Architettura Per il Design." *l'Arca* (September 1987), pp. 30–38. (International Design Center)

Vogel, Carol. "Changes of Pace." *New York Times* (November 24, 1985), pp. 122–127. (Spielberg Apartment One)

Vogel, Carol. "Inside Art." *New York Times* (June 21, 1996). (Museum of Contemporary Art)

Warchol, Paul. "Designing for Themselves: Charles Gwathmey, Marrio Botta, Design Collective." *Interior Design* (vol. 63, no. 05, March 1992), pp. 117–121. (Gwathmey Apartment)

Webb, Michael. *Architects House Themselves.* New York: The Preservation Press, 1995, pp. 182–186. (Gwathmey Apartment)

Weber, Bruce. "Moving Bits, Bytes and Books to the Library of the Future." *New York Times* (Metro section, April 5, 1996). (Science, Industry and Business Library)

Werk, Bauen+Wohnen (March 3, 1994), pp. 68–69. (Zumikon Residence)

"What Wright has Wrought." *Metropolis* (vol. 06, no. 08, April 1987), pp. 20–21. (Solomon R. Guggenheim Museum Addition, Renovation, and Restoration)

"Wright Despues de Wright: Museo Guggenheim, Nueva York, Gwathmey Siegel." *A & V* (vol. 64, no. 01, January 1993), pp. 84–99. (Solomon R. Guggenheim Museum Addition, Renovation, and Restoration)

"Wright Revamped: Solomon R. Guggenheim Museum Restoration and Expansion, New York City, Gwathmey Siegel & Associates Architects." *Architecture* (vol. 81, no. 08, August 1992). (Solomon R. Guggenheim Museum Addition, Renovation, and Restoration)

"Wright Wronged: Gwathmey Siegel's Proposed Guggenheim Addition Raises Crucial Questions about the Museum's Role as Cultural Caretaker." *House & Garden* (vol. 158, no. 02, February 1986), pp. 42–48. (Solomon R. Guggenheim Museum Addition, Renovation, and Restoration)

Yee, Roger. "Having it All." *Contract Design* (March 1993), pp. 42–48. (Capital Group Inc. Offices)

Zevon, Susan. *Inside Architecture.* Massachusetts: Rockport Publishers, 1996, pp. 74–81. (Gwathmey Apartment)

Selected Awards & Exhibitions

Awards

Award of Excellence in Recognition of Distinguished Accomplishment in Library Architecture
American Institute of Architects and American Library Association
Science, Industry and Business Library
New York Public Library
New York, New York
1997

Record Interiors
Architectural Record
Science, Industry and Business Library
New York Public Library
New York, New York
1996

Award of Excellence
Architectural Commission, Claremont, California
Pitzer College Academic Buildings
Claremont, California
1996

Design Award
American Institute of Architects,
New York Chapter
Solomon R. Guggenheim Museum
Addition, Renovation and Restoration
New York, New York
1995

Record House
Architectural Record
Zumikon Residence
Zumikon, Switzerland
1995

Distinguished Architecture Award
American Institute of Architects,
New York Chapter
Opel Residence
Shelburne, Vermont
1992

Distinguished Architecture Award
American Institute of Architects,
New York Chapter
Contemporary Resort Convention Center,
Walt Disney World
Lake Buena Vista, Florida
1992

Distinguished Architecture Award
American Institute of Architects,
New York Chapter
College of Agriculture and Life Sciences
Cornell University
Ithaca, New York
1991

Lifetime Achievement Award
New York State Association of Architects
1990

Honor Award
American Institute of Architects,
North Carolina Chapter
Thomas I. Storrs Architecture Building
University of North Carolina at Charlotte
Charlotte, North Carolina
1990

National Honor Award
American Institute of Architects
Library and Science Building
Westover School
Middlebury, Connecticut
1988

Record House
Architectural Record
Garey Residence
Kent, Connecticut
1988

Record House
Architectural Record
Opel Residence
Shelburne, Vermont
1988

Excellence in Design Award
Art Commission of the City of New York
East Academic Complex
Eugenio Maria de Hostos Community College
Bronx, New York
1988

Record House
Architectural Record
Spielberg Residence
East Hampton, New York
1988

Bard Award
City Club of New York
International Design Centers I & II
Long Island City, New York
1988

Distinguished Architecture Award
American Institute of Architects,
New York Chapter
Library and Science Building
Westover School
Middlebury, Connecticut
1987

Award of Excellence
American Library Association
Library and Science Building
Westover School
Middlebury, Connecticut
1987

Design Award
Interiors
International Design Centers I & II
Long Island City, New York
1987

Design Award
New York State Association of Architects
International Design Centers I & II
Long Island City, New York
1987

Certificate of Merit
Municipal Art Society of New York
International Design Centers I & II
Long Island City, New York
1986

Unbuilt Project Award
American Institute of Architects,
New York Chapter
College of Agriculture and Life Sciences
Cornell University
Ithaca, New York
1986

Distinguished Architecture Award
American Institute of Architects,
Connecticut Chapter
Library and Science Building
Westover School
Middlebury, Connecticut
1986

Distinguished Architecture Award
American Institute of Architects,
New York Chapter
deMenil Residence
East Hampton, New York
1985

Honor Award
American Society of Landscape Architects
deMenil Residence
East Hampton, New York
1985

Distinguished Architecture Award
American Institute of Architects,
New York Chapter
Arango Apartment
New York, New York
1985

Record Interior
Architectural Record
Spielberg Apartment
New York, New York
1985

Record Interior
Architectural Record
Arango Apartment
New York, New York
1984

Design Award
New York State Association of Architects
Library and Science Building
Westover School
Middlebury, Connecticut
1984

Distinguished Architecture Award
American Institute of Architects,
New York Chapter
First City Bank
Houston, Texas
1984

National Honor Award
American Institute of Architects
Taft Residence
Cincinnati, Ohio
1984

Design Award
New York State Association of Architects
deMenil Residence
East Hampton, New York
1984

Medal of Honor
American Institute of Architects,
New York Chapter
1983

Design Award
Interiors
Gwathmey Siegel & Associates Architects
Offices
New York, New York
1983

Firm Award
American Institute of Architects
1982

Record Interior
Architectural Record
Morton L. Janklow & Associates Offices
New York, New York
1982

Design Award
Progressive Architecture
deMenil Residence
East Hampton, New York
1982

Design Award
American Institute of Architects,
Los Angeles Chapter
deMenil Residence
Santa Monica, California
1982

Distinguished Architecture Award
American Institute of Architects,
New York Chapter
Viereck Residence
Amagansett, New York
1982

Record House
Architectural Record
Viereck Residence
Amagansett, New York
1982

Design Award
Progressive Architecture
Wick Alumni Center
University of Nebraska
Lincoln, Nebraska
1982

Product Design Award
Institute of Business Designers
Desks and Credenza System
Knoll International
1982

Exhibitions

Stung by Splendor: Working Drawings and the Creative Moment
Cooper Union for the Advancement of Science and Art
New York, New York
September 1997

Five Architects—Twenty Years Later
University of Maryland School of Architecture
College Park, Maryland
November 1992

Architects for Snoopy
Montreal Museum of Fine Arts
Montreal, Canada
January 1992

The Guggenheim Museum, New York City: The Addition, Renovation, Expansion, and Restoration by Gwathmey Siegel & Associates Architects
Harvard University Graduate School of Design
Cambridge, Massachusetts
September 1991

Charles Gwathmey and Robert Siegel Architects, New York: Recent Work
Architektur Forum Zurich
Zurich, Switzerland
May 1991

Charles Gwathmey and Robert Siegel: Projects and Furniture for Knoll
Knoll International
Tokyo, Japan
April 1990

New York Architektur, 1970–1990
Deutches Architektur Museum
Frankfurt, Germany
April 1988

Architects Design Birdhouses
Parrish Art Museum
Southhampton, New York
May 1987

Modern Redux: Critical Alternatives for Architecture in the Next Decade
Grey Art Gallery and Study Center
New York University
New York, New York
March 1986

Toad Hall, East Hampton, New York
Institute for Architecture and Urban Studies
(de Menil Residence, East Hampton)
New York, New York
January 1983

Five Houses, Gwathmey Siegel Architects
Institute for Architecture and Urban Studies
New York, New York
December 1977

Another Chance for Housing: Low-rise Alternative
Museum of Modern Art
New York, New York
June 1973

State University College at Purchase, New York
Museum of Modern Art
New York, New York
April 1971

The Architecture of Suffolk County
Heckscher Museum
May 1971

Retrospective 1968
Princeton University
Princeton, New Jersey
November 1968

40 under 40
Architectural League of New York
New York, New York
September 1966

7 Architects and 7 Sculptors
School of Visual Arts
New York, New York
November 1967

Acknowledgments

We would like to thank all the architects who have collaborated with us over the years, as well as our clients for their trust and loyalty, and Kate Stirling who made this monograph a reality.'

Charles Gwathmey and Robert Siegel

Photography credits

Peter Aaron/Esto: 57 (2,3); 59 (10–12); 130 (2); 131 (3); 132 (4,5); 133 (9,10); 134 (11–13); 135 (14,15)

Assassi Productions: 86 (2,3); 87 (4,5); 88 (8–10); 89 (11–15); 126 (4); 127 (8); 129 (14); 140 (1); 141 (3–5); 143 (9,10); 144 (11); 145 (12); 147 (15,16); 148 (17); 149 (18); 150 (19,20); 151 (21,22); 152 (26,27); 154 (30–32); 157 (38,40); 160 (1–3); 161 (6); 162 (7,8); 163 (9,10); 165 (14–16); 166 (21,22); 167 (23–25); 168 (26–28); 169 (29); 190 (2); 191 (3); 192 (4,5); 193 (10,11); 194 (12–14); 196 (15–18); 197 (19); 202 (1), 203 (2–5); 204 (8,9); 205 (10,11)

Tom Bonner: 120 (1); 121 (2,3); 122 (6); 123 (7–9); 211 (4); 212 (5,6); 213 (7)

Steven Brooke Studios: 174 (2); 175 (3,4,6); 176 (7,8);177 (9,10)

Richard Bryant/Arcaid: 29 (4–8); 30 (9–12); 31 (14); 48 (1); 49 (3–5); 50 (8); 51 (9–11); 68 (2); 69 (4,5); 70 (10); 72 (16); 73 (17); 74 (2); 75 (3–5); 76 (6–9); 77 (10); 106 (2); 110 (10); 111 (13–16)

Bernstein Associates/Harrison, NY: 209 (7,8)

Jeff Goldberg/Esto: 18 (3,4); 20 (6,7,9); 22 (2); 23 (3); 24 (4,5); 25 (6); 27 (9–12); 34 (7); 35 (10); 36 (1,2); 37 (3,4); 38 (8,12); 39 (13–15); 52 (1,2); 53 (3,5–7); 54 (8–11); 55 (13–15); 56 (1); 57 (4); 59 (9); 60 (2); 61 (3–5); 62 (9–13); 63 (14,15); 102 (2); 103 (3–5); 104 (6–8)

David Hewitt/Anne Garrison: 126 (2,3); 127 (5–7); 128 (11–13)

Glen Hitchcox: 32 (2)

Timothy Hursley 33 (1–3); 34 (5-8); 35 (11); 37 (5); 38 (7); 40 (1–3); 41 (5); 42 (6–8); 43 (9); 72 (13,14)

Barbara Karant: 45 (3); 46 (4–6); 47 (8)

Elliott Kaufman: 82 (1,2); 83 (3–5); 84 (6–8); 85 (11)

Norman McGrath: 16 (1)

Jock Pottle/Esto: 113 (3); 115 (8); 136 (2); 137 (4); 138 (10); 139 (11); 159 (6–8); 170 (2); 171 (3); 173 (8,9); 198 (3,4); 199 (5,6); 206 (1,2); 215 (6,8,9); 218 (2,3); 219 (7–9); 221 (15–17)

David Ramsey: 64 (2); 67 (10)

Durston Saylor: 186 (2); 187 (3); 188 (4–6); 189 (7,8)

Gordon Schenck: 65 (3,4); 66 (7); 67 (8,9,11)

Skyviews: 68 (1)

Luca Vignelli: 244; 245

Paul Warchol: 20 (8); 78 (2); 79 (4,5); 80 (8–10); 81 (11); 90 (2); 91 (3–6); 92 (7); 93 (10–13); 95 (17); 96 (2); 97 (3); 98 (4–7); 99 (8); 116 (1,2); 117 (4); 118 (5,6); 119 (7); 124 (1–3); 125 (5)

All other photography courtesy of Gwathmey Siegel & Associates Architects

Index

Bold page numbers refer to projects
included in Selected and Current Works